‘Can there still be experiences of purposeful encounters at the heart of psychotherapy in our era when manualised approaches are increasingly being given primacy? This remarkable book sets out to show the detrimental effects of psychotherapy in general of the systemisation of calculable techniques when coupled with changes in cultural practice, political priorities, and economic pressures. Patricia Talens, a master theoretician and importantly practitioner in the field, cogently argues that this has resulted in a diminution of psychotherapies that require intuition and situational attunement as ethical endeavours; this has radically reduced, and continues to reduce, diversity in psychotherapeutic practices and research.’

Prof Del Loewenthal, *Emeritus Professor of Psychotherapy & Counselling, University of Roehampton; Chair, Southern Association for Psychotherapy and Counselling (SAFPAC)*

EMBRACING COMPLEXITY

Embracing Complexity: A Critical Approach to Efficacy and Manualised Practices in Psychotherapy considers the implications for psychotherapeutic practice and research when these are required to demonstrate 'efficacy' through repeatable models and manualised practices. This book discusses how manualised treatments impact the therapist and their practice with clients, challenging the notion that measuring and repeating manualised psychotherapeutic practice always moves toward best practice.

It considers the growth of manualised interventions such as cognitive behavioural therapy (CBT) which have undergone rapid expansion and implementation in recent decades and are often regarded as the gold standard of measurable, evidence-based treatment. However, manualised practices may be critiqued as reductive and failing to incorporate the complexities of the self as a whole into the therapeutic relationship, instead over-relying on the reduction of symptoms relating to one diagnosis. This book considers whether standardisation in psychotherapeutic research and practice can sacrifice key therapeutic and relational elements in the name of conformity and how training and standardisation can monopolise the psychotherapeutic space. Adopting a critical psychological approach, this book explores the current situation in psychology, showcases the voice of different practitioners, and explores what is gained and what is lost through the increasing adoption of manualised therapies.

By pointing out alternative paths for therapists that emerge from a fuller and unfiltered understanding of the psychotherapeutic space, this book will be of great interest to students and researchers in the areas of psychotherapy, critical psychology, and phenomenological studies, and to mental health professionals and trainees.

Patricia Talens is an existential analytic psychotherapist, a supervisor, and a researcher working both privately and within the charity sector in London and Brighton. Her PhD specialised in research examining how therapists interact with techniques in their practice and how technique and method in psychotherapy can shape therapists.

Concepts for Critical Psychology: Disciplinary Boundaries Re-thought

Series editor: Ian Parker

Developments inside psychology that question the history of the discipline and the way it functions in society have led many psychologists to look outside the discipline for new ideas. This series draws on cutting edge critiques from just outside psychology in order to complement and question critical arguments emerging inside. The authors provide new perspectives on subjectivity from disciplinary debates and cultural phenomena adjacent to traditional studies of the individual.

The books in the series are useful for advanced level undergraduate and postgraduate students, researchers and lecturers in psychology and other related disciplines such as cultural studies, geography, literary theory, philosophy, psychotherapy, social work and sociology.

Most recently published titles:

Liberation Psychology and Refusal
Confronting Capitalist Alienation, Ideology, and Nature
Nick Malherbe

The Great Resignation as Neoliberal Compliance and Critique
A Foucauldian Analysis
Caroline Austin

Embracing Complexity
A Critical Approach to Efficacy and Manualised Practices in Psychotherapy
Patricia Talens

For more information about this series, please visit: www.routledge.com/Concepts-for-Critical-Psychology/book-series/CONCEPTSCRIT

EMBRACING COMPLEXITY

A Critical Approach to Efficacy and Manualised Practices in Psychotherapy

Patricia Talens

Routledge
Taylor & Francis Group
LONDON AND NEW YORK

Designed cover image: Getty Images @Eoneren

First published 2027
by Routledge
4 Park Square, Milton Park, Abingdon, Oxon OX14 4RN

and by Routledge
605 Third Avenue, New York, NY 10158

Routledge is an imprint of the Taylor & Francis Group, an informa business

British Library Cataloguing-in-Publication Data
A catalogue record for this book is available from the British Library

ISBN: 9781041096900 (hbk)
ISBN: 9781041096887 (pbk)
ISBN: 9781003651666 (ebk)

DOI: 10.4324/9781003651666

Typeset in Times New Roman
by codeMantra

CONTENTS

ACKNOWLEDGEMENTS

A special thank you to Prof. Del Loewenthal, Dr. Onel Brooks, Dr. Julia Cayne, Julia Utting and Dr. James Davies for your insights, time, and support and for facilitating a learning community that encourages people to challenge and push their work ever further. Your guidance has not only provided a safe environment for creativity but also the courage to always break through. A huge thank you to Prof. Ian Parker for your kind encouragement and for helping this book become a reality. A big thank you to friends and peers at the University of Roehampton and SAFPAC for your ongoing support and open conversations and to Laura Merrifield for being the backbone of the PhD community at Roehampton.

An enormous thank you to all the practitioners who offered their time and experiences for the purposes of the research and this book; without you, this would not have been possible. Thank you to the people who have entered the therapy space with me over the years and who embark on their courageous journeys whilst letting me learn with them. Thank you to friends and family who have offered unwavering support and to my wonderful partner and brujas for your endless encouragement and for never failing to show up. And finally, my endless gratitude goes to Elizabeth Meakins – thank you for your wise and generous lessons in the poetics of therapy.

SERIES PREFACE

A Critical Approach to Efficacy and Manualised Practices in Psychotherapy

The discipline of psychology is often accused, by critical psychologists, of 'reductionism', of the reduction to the level of the individual of social processes, or, also often, of a reduction to that level from neurophysiology. Psychologists are obsessed with their own domain of analysis, their own favourite object of study, the individual. However, the turn towards qualitative research in recent years has drawn attention to another, no less important, reductive procedure in mainstream psychology, the reduction of the contradictoriness and messiness of the human condition to numbers, to so-called 'data' – itself a representation of reality – to quantification. This reductive error inside psychology then feeds into forms of psychotherapy that psychologists are keen on guiding, particularly cognitive behavioural therapy (CBT). Here, the error is not only conceptual but plays out in the lives of clients. Disregard for societal context, misunderstanding of the nature of the bodily material grounding of distress, and avoidance of complexity becomes the very substance of psychologised psychotherapy and manualised practice.

This book takes another tack, which is in tune with methodological advances in psychology and in psychotherapeutic research by seeking to 'embrace complexity' and thereby enable sustained attention to the embedded social lives of clients and, as this book particularly emphasises, therapists. Patricia Talens shows us that this sustained attention in phenomenological enquiry can also be rigorous and illuminating. This critical approach to positivist reductionist quantitative psychology and its spawn and helpmeet in CBT has far-reaching consequences that are explored in the course of this book. Conceptually rich yet highly practical, this book tells us about the philosophical resources that phenomenological approaches in psychotherapeutic research have themselves embraced and honed into useful method, and it puts that method to work.

In this way, this book throws light on contemporary attempts to manualise psychotherapy, the way these manualised approaches distort and reduce the particular journey that a psychotherapist has taken into their practice, the specific qualities of the therapeutic interaction and so the singular experience and life goals of a client. The distortion is both systematic and chaotic, and once a manualised approach is put to work, it is difficult to undo the damage that can be caused, not only in the misrepresentation of a client's life in case reports and academic texts but also in the prescription of desired 'outcomes' of the therapy itself.

The foundational claim of manualised psychotherapy – that it is more effective – is carefully and necessarily intricately unravelled in this book. Efficacy is the terrible twin of manualised practice, promising what it cannot deliver: neat and tidy outcomes, data that confirm its own presuppositions, and representations of psychotherapy that cover over the cracks and contradictions in human subjectivity. This book takes us into the lived experience of therapists who are encountering the increasingly intensive and pervasive audit culture of health services, and it steps back from those phenomenological accounts to contextualise and evaluate what these therapists are being subjected to. This book is in line with critical psychological research practice to take us into a phenomenon and allow us to locate it, to be both inside and outside it, 'outwith' psychology.

Ian Parker
University of Manchester

1

INTRODUCTION

The objective accent falls on WHAT is said, the subjective accent on HOW it is said.
(Kierkegaard)

Psychotherapy can often feel caught in the tension between care and control as practitioners navigate tending to human suffering whilst trying to account for it. At the heart of psychotherapy sits an experience of a purposeful encounter between two or more people in a shared space over time. Whilst the purpose of such an encounter is shaped by the style and modality a therapist brings and the narrative of the client, this has traditionally been a space in which countless possibilities can emerge in conversation. However, despite the richness and depth of thought in theory and practice regarding the ways in which psychotherapy is carried out, it continues to undergo a process of systemisation which increasingly answers to the demands of quantifiable 'evidence' (Wampold et al., 2017; Waller, Stringer and Mayer, 2012). The trajectory of which is an "…increasingly sophisticated calculus of efficiency and economy in assembling means towards ends" (Dunne, 1993. p. 177).

In recent decades there has been a dominant shift towards manualised practices becoming overwhelmingly favoured and most widely used in the industry of funded therapies (Dalal, 2018; Güven and Gökçe, 2018). This has led to the widespread use of therapeutic practices which adhere to and derive from partial or wholly pre-designed manuals and agendas which are set outside of the therapeutic context before the first word is uttered. This prompts us to consider the implications for psychotherapy and research when complexity is reduced to an applicable methodology. Despite challenges towards the notion that 'efficacy' and 'evidence' within psychotherapy are objectively sound and always move towards a better practice, manualised approaches have gained traction over frameworks which prioritise the relational and contextual. One possible explanation is that evidence-based paradigms better integrate and serve neoliberal values and bureaucratic systems which have come to frame access to care. This book considers this possibility and asks why there is an

DOI: 10.4324/9781003651666-1

increasingly exclusive focus on measurable outcomes and efficiency. This is not in opposition to evidence and accountability, rather from a concern that we risk a narrowing view of how we understand psychotherapy and all its potentiality. When we organise around objective interpretations which lend themselves to what can be counted and compared, we lose sight of how something is expressed and experienced within this relational practice. And whilst measurement can inform us and is useful in many ways, it cannot fully grasp or capture the ways in which both the therapist and client may be changed by the encounter itself.

To begin exploring these questions, we need to take stock of a broader picture and see how the nexus of cultural practice, political priorities, economic pressures, and calculable techniques all come together and seep into the way psychotherapy is practised and evaluated. What becomes of interest are the ordering and shaping forces which sit behind the current picture we have of psychotherapy. Recently, many psychotherapeutic debates are centred towards specific models of practice and research. The focus here is to try and shed light on how a network of calculus and technological efficiency influence the emergence of these models and shape our understanding of what psychotherapy is and what it does. The implication is that modern systems in professional practices such as psychotherapy increasingly treat interventions as a potential technical avenue for optimisation.

Taking the view that psychotherapeutic technique is a technological matter in which an instrumental design is deployed and applied, what are the implications for psychotherapy as an ethical endeavour which requires intuition and situational attunement? Viewing technique as a form of technology widens our traditional understanding from the instrumental to one which is also anthropological. We move beyond discussions of physical technologies to conversations about the way the technical helps drive efficient outcomes and steer clear of uncertainty. This prompts an exploration of how an increase in procedural and technical thinking shapes and mediates the therapeutic encounter for the therapist and their clients. Positioning the capacity to be technical in the therapy room as one potentiality of how a therapist might show up draws the question of why we choose this mode. What draws therapists towards manualised practice and how does high levels of application impact the therapeutic space? In addition, are there social, economic, and political agendas which call upon therapists to be technical and maximise metric outcomes? If so, then it is imperative that we become clear of the implications.

This book hopes to serve as kindling to ignite larger, more nuanced conversations about external factors which shape what happens in the therapy room. Factors which are entangled with the political, social, economic, and technological landscape. It asks how this entanglement can subtly reshape and alter the ways in which therapists show up to the therapeutic encounter.

The book is not aimed at evidencing one way or the other about a particular technique, rather it takes the position that the systemisation of technique threatens diversity in practice and research. The aim is to better understand how different levels of manualisation impact the therapist and their practice. Addressing how standardisation in psychotherapeutic research and practice can create a 'Procrustean bed' which sacrifices key therapeutic and relational elements in the name of conformity. Furthermore, we ask whether a crisis point has been reached in psychotherapy, when standardisation, and professionalisation monopolise the psychotherapeutic space rather than the experience which emerges in the therapy room.

Presented, is the view that manualised interventions and techniques are not static, disconnected tools, but rather, they contribute and serve economic, social and political structures. Structures which at times, prioritise measurement and outcome scales over quality of care. But how did we get here and why do we keep drifting towards evermore manualised care despite the warnings of what might be lost?

As restrictions to models and research tighten, we begin to see how highly bureaucratic stages of development threaten creativity and, in turn, risk a self-promoting industry (Davies, 2009). Furthermore, therapists exposed to highly monitored institutions such as NHS Talking Therapies (previously known as IAPT) are impacted by extensive monitoring practices which have come to undermine psychotherapeutic care for people. We begin to see how the emergence of an audit culture and the managerialism of care create a tension for practitioners between caring for people and meeting their targets. This has led to a factory style working environment which has swept through certain institutions (Bruun, 2023).

With this in mind, we must ask, might this be too high of a cost when we consider the growing body of work which stipulates how variation in treatment models has little impact or effect on improving outcomes in psychotherapy (Brown, Dreis and Nace, 1999; Wampold et al., 1997). Instead, disadvantages are encountered as treatment *manuals provide an inadequate representation of psychotherapy* because they treat interventions as independent of the therapists and clients involved in the therapeutic process (Duncan and Miller, 2006). Furthermore, there is controversy regarding models based on 'efficacy' and effectiveness' in psychotherapy due to researchers struggling to agree on a clear assessment of what is valuable within therapeutic interventions (Nathan, 2007), which in turn prompts a call for increased contextual models in psychotherapeutic research (Wampold et al., 2017).

Understanding the shift towards predetermined interventions and the culture of evidence-based practice and research feels paramount but is also a complex task. The priority here is to introduce a discussion on four key areas which give an essence of the altered balance towards systematised ways of working and thinking. Whilst each chapter will have a central focus, the philosophy of technology runs throughout the book, offering a thread which brings together many moving parts. This is to centralise the idea of how technology and technique play a core role in the way we condition enquiry and how this enquiry may in turn condition us. Through critical theory and existential and phenomenological philosophy, the chapters can open the conversation and incorporate political and social commentary regarding the use of technologies for efficiency and how this shapes culture.

There are three core intentions for the book. Firstly, to challenge the notion that measuring and repeating manualised psychotherapeutic practice always moves towards best practice. Secondly, to address how standardisation in psychotherapeutic research and practice can sacrifice key therapeutic and relational elements in the name of conformity. And thirdly, to better understand how manualised treatments impact the therapist and their practice with clients.

The Chapters

The first exploration is the tilt from ***'Implication to Application'***. Introducing the relationship between means and ends, by drawing on ancient Greek and contemporary understanding of technology so that the developments and changes can be better understood. In doing so, the nuances and changes between the term 'technology' and Technê can be fully appreciated. Introduced is the topology of phronesis, praxis, and poesis to help deconstruct some of our perceptions and ideas of what technology means. How we have come to know it fundamentally as an instrumental object rather than part of our own 'Being' (Stiegler, 1994). Through Aristotle's ethics we see these terms become categorised into forms of knowledge and undergo conceptualisation (Jaffa, 1952).

The chapter further explores the impact of the Enlightenment and how the rise of science brings about a further narrowing of Technê as we enter a rational and productive form of making. By the 21st century, we see science shapes the discipline of psychology and the emergence of manualised practices referred to as a technology of change. This sets the foundation and context to the way in which the cultural movement of terminology and understanding has shifted towards a different encounter with the idea of Technê. Further exploring the rise of manualised practice and the implications this has on how we understand psychotherapy, highlighting the fluid nature of cultural practices and how the evidence-based industry is evolving through calculative thinking (Dalal, 2018).

'Theory to Calculation' explores the infrastructure of funded therapies as a system which regulates better with manualised practices. How the use of 'randomised controlled trials' (RCTs) within the medical model is applied to psychotherapy and as such becomes a politically convenient form of technology (Guilfoyle, 2008).

The relationship between capitalism and efficiency is explored through the work of Max Weber and Mark Fisher to highlight the unseen but influential backdrop that feeds into decision-making. This demonstrates that the culture is shaped not only by historical and visible events but also by thinking, beliefs, and modes of being which manifest in visible actions and choices. Exploring Martin Heidegger's warning that we become caught up in system if we are not aware of the non-visible essence which guides the process and in turn, can engulf us in a mode of 'Being'.

Further Heideggerian notions such as 'bringing-forth', 'challenging-forth', 'standing reserve', and 'enframing' are discussed further in relation to the propelling nature of technology and how it becomes a form of concealment.

'Discovery to Evidence' which explores the nature of research and how specification and 'efficacy' are not always the best frameworks by which to understand relational and complex phenomena. Also how prioritising the demonstrable often leads to a restriction in discovery and diminishes fluidity in practice and research, particularly because broader agendas privilege 'evidence' over more pluralistic approaches towards enquiring (Feyerabend, 2010). The outcome of calculative and meditative thinking is explored for psychotherapeutic research and practice. We see psychotherapy moving towards monitoring and instructing practice which fits rather than promoting critical engagement with philosophical and ethical underpinnings. This cultural shift towards a calculative and measurable understanding of people's experiences raises a question regarding the nature of knowledge and ethical stance in psychotherapy (Miller, 2004). It draws into question which types of knowledge are valued in the field of psychotherapy, and the ethical stance the therapist and client find themselves in when governed by systems designed for efficiency and standardisation.

'Clinician to Technician' considers the impact on therapists and their sense of self with manualised interventions. It probes into the complexities which arise when there is an over-manualisation in their restrictive nature which can impact the responsiveness of the therapist in real time and situation (Marshall, 2009). The chapter therefore considers the importance of therapeutic paradigms which explore the capacity to 'be with' rather than 'doing to' as a source of ethics, learning, and development in psychotherapy.

Returning to the philosophy of technology, Don Ihde (1990) and Peter-Paul Verbeek's (2016) post-phenomenological theory of 'mediation' is introduced to offer a framework to explore these implications. As 'mediation theory' is orientated around understanding how technologies shape and mediate our experience, its framework allows for a pragmatic approach to understanding the first-hand experience of these technologies from the perspective of therapists. This brings to the forefront an understanding of how these technologies in the form of manualised interventions impact the relationship and space between client and therapist.

'What Therapists Say' focuses on the descriptive experiences of 12 therapists and their relationship with manualised practice, and implications are brought to light for the therapist and their work. This chapter explores the ways in which manualised practice shapes the internal and external world of the therapist and how claims of evidence-based knowledge have altered the ways in which therapists respond within the therapeutic encounter. It also highlights the importance of acknowledging our relationship with method and technique as part of an ethical engagement with our practice.

Approaching these questions from a qualitative and discovery-orientated standpoint allows for feedback that sits beyond metric outcomes. By doing so, it allows us a return to conversation and exploration, to nuance and fluidity, to changed meaning and reconstituting ourselves and relationships; all of which I argue sit as central components of the therapeutic endeavour but which have come under attack in the name of 'efficacy'.

Who Is This Book for

If this book sits in your hand or appears on your screen, you are likely already connected to the psychotherapeutic world in some way. Perhaps you are a practitioner, trainee, student, researcher, or supervisor. You may have been a client or thinking of starting your own journey in therapy or simply curious about psychotherapy. Whichever seat you occupy, this book has been written to help illuminate some of the ways in which the world outside the therapy room inevitably shapes what happens inside.

This book is intended to offer an alternative position, one from the experiences and voices of those practising at the very centre without a drive to evidence or produce an outcome. It simply allows practitioners to speak of their experiences and to reconnect psychotherapy as an experiential practice as well as an intellectual one.

Taking Up a Position

It is perhaps helpful here to offer both my theoretical position and my personal position towards the writing. From a theoretical perspective, my practice as a psychotherapist, supervisor, and researcher is labelled as integrative but from a phenomenological standing. This in some way means my work is rooted in philosophy and ethics and led by practice, bringing experience, uncertainty, and relational depth to the forefront. By drawing on phenomenological thought, there is an opportunity to resist abstraction, not as a rejection but as a clearing of space for embodied, ethical, and relational ways of knowing to emerge. It is through these vantage points that I increasingly come to experience psychotherapy as an art form in which we reimagine our stories and discover the possibilities that live within us. This is not a denial of theory or technique, rather a recognition there is always a great deal more available to the therapeutic encounter than any one theory or metric measure.

Perhaps most importantly, I too sat as a client, and it was not a flawless application of techniques which were the most transformative moments. Rather it was the ruptures, compassion, mistrust, frustration, laughter, affection, repair, and so much more which became the very foundation of the work. And all of which, whilst potentially predictable in some ways, cannot be anticipated in a mechanical manner but instead responded to in context and time. Even with theory present, it served the relationship rather than directing or dominating it. Such responsiveness might appear fragile and easily undermined if therapy is required to conform to a predetermined agenda set outside of the room and outside of the context.

A Couple of Clarifying Points

The complexity of these issues far exceeds what any single book can resolve or describe. What this book hopes to do is gently start conversations and bring together thoughts from ethics, philosophy, literature, practice, and theory to question what we think we know. The book is to be used as a platform from which to discover and ask more questions about psychotherapy. As such, it does not seek to answer but instead offer possible interpretations of why manualisation has become so dominant in the field.

The mention of cognitive behavioural therapy (CBT) or other forms of manualised practice is *not* intended as a critique of the approach; those discussions will be left to others who are more versed on the subject matter. These approaches, especially CBT, are brought in as examples of deep and rich theory which over time have been tuned to fast paced and simplified versions for economic demand. This book adopts a ‘critical psychological’ approach in its practice by returning to discovery-orientated dialogue. It explores the current situation in psychology, not through measurement or with an agenda to pit methods against each other, nor does it seek to prove or disprove what works. Rather it simply asks how and what these practitioners in frontline services experience in their practice. The book is attempting to demonstrate how any theory can over time be transitioned from complex thought to simplistic application and how that can serve institutions over people.

The term 'psychotherapy' is used as an umbrella term throughout the book and is interchangeable with the words manualised therapy and practice. It is used to encompass all the psychotherapeutic practices and falls into different paradigms as opposed to one definition. By removing the restrictions of what is and isn't psychotherapeutic research and practice, the book can move freely across multiple disciplines such as literature, science, philosophy, art, and countless frameworks of therapy. The purpose of this is to position psychotherapy and what psychotherapy does as a complex task and endeavour which alters and shifts depending on situation, time, place, and paradigm. This helps facilitate an open conversation rather than start from a defined and comparative criteria. Again, the ethos of the book is not a *'for'* or *'against'* argument but rather a conversation which allows a nuanced understanding of how we interact with technique.

While this book focuses primarily within the context of the United Kingdom, its theoretical concerns are globally relevant. Across much of the world, psychotherapy is situated within cultures governed by ideas of efficiency and productivity which have economic implications. Outcomes are prioritised but rarely is there a space to ask what kind of outcomes matter? The quality of the work and the lived realities of clinicians often remain largely absent from the ways success is measured. This book hopes to rectify that by offering the experiences of therapists as an account of the way technique is encountered in practice.

This is not about taking one side over the other despite my own theoretical orientations aligning with a phenomenological grounding. For even in phenomenology and existentialism, there too can come about a systemisation of its core theories. Rather, this is about addressing the balance by becoming aware of some of the shaping factors which impact the therapy space and which are not easily visible.

An Orientation in Phenomenological Language

'Abjection' orientated towards the visceral horror when encountering or confronting that which disrupts identity and the boundaries of the self, repressed in a "corporeal reality" (Kristeva, 1982).

'Bad Faith' refers to a form of self-deception in which a person denies the freedom they hold by adopting values and beliefs about the world and themselves from the social. It is a self-deception which holds on to a set of feelings and can view itself as a 'thing' that does not have the freedom to change (Sartre, 1956).

'Being' is considered in its Heideggerian context (1962) and is that which lays the ontological foundation from which *'Dasein'* emerges. It is indefinable to the logical and transcends categorical distinction. It is the ground of existence that precedes all 'being'. In essence, once it becomes something, it no longer sits as *'Being'*.

'Dasein' is the human mode of *'Being'* which is aware and understands its existence but this understanding in some way contributes and shapes its very being in the world. It is from *'Being'* which is already making the world and being made by the world; therefore, Dasein is the inseparability of *'Being'* and the world (Heidegger, 1962).

'Enframing' is the Heideggerian term in which we frame a particular encounter so that something shows up from us in a particular way (Heidegger, 1977).

'House of being' refers to another Heideggerian (2012) concept in which he articulates that language is the house of being and so the language we use in some way situates us in a form of dwelling.

'Intentionality' is rooted in Husserl's (2014) work within phenomenology which can be understood as a consciousness of something other than itself and, as such, a directiveness towards something or about something. This changes throughout the course of the study. The reason for this is that Heidegger's version explores 'intentionality' not as a cognition but as an action rather than thinking.

'Mediation' is considered in a post-phenomenological context which takes technology as a mediator between being and the world. Therefore, our experience is shaped by technology rather than by reality (Ihde, 1990).

'Other' is used in relation to Emmanuel Lévinas (1967) as that which ungraspable and which calls upon us an ethical demand to respond. For Léevinas, the 'Other' is unknowable and cannot be made into any form of knowable object.

'Technologies of self' is considered in relation to Michel Foucault's (1994) methods and techniques which individuals practise in constituting themselves.

'World of Appearances' is related to Hannah Arendt's world of plurality in which we always appear and therefore we not only perceive the world but are also perceived by the world. It is the public sphere which is called 'the political'. Hence for Arendt, *'Being'* and *'Appearance'* coincide and hold a relationship (Arendt, 1971).

References

Arendt, H. (1971). *The life of the mind.* Ed. M. McCarthy. San Diego, CA: Mariner Books.

Brown, J. Dreis, S. Nace, D. K. (1999). What really makes a difference in psychotherapy outcome? Why does managed care want to know? In: Hubble, M. A. Duncan, B. L. Miller, S. D. (Eds.), *The heart and soul of change: What works in therapy*, pp. 389–406. Washington, DC: American Psychological Association.

Bruun, K. M. (2023). A factory of therapy: Accountability and the monitoring of psychological therapy in IAPT. *Anthropology and Medicine*. Vol. 30 (4), pp. 313–329.

Dalal, F. (2018). *CBT: The cognitive behavioural tsunami. Managerialism, politics and the corruptions of science*. New York: Routledge.

Davies, J. (2009). Psychotherapy and the third wave of professionalisation. *European Journal of Psychotherapy and Counselling*. Vol. 11 (2), pp. 191–202.

Duncan, B. L. Miller, S. D. (2005). *Treatment manuals do not improve outcomes*. In: Norcross, J. Levant, R. Beutler, L. (2005) (Eds.), *Evidence-based practices in mental health: Debate and dialogue on the fundamental questions*. Washington, DC: American Psychological Association Press, pp. 140–149.

Dunne, J. (1993). *Back to the rough ground: Practical judgment and the lure of technique*. IN: University of Notre Dame. Indiana USA.

Feyerabend, P. (2010). *Against method*. London: New Left Books.

Foucault, M. (1994). *Michel Foucault power: Essential works of Foucault 1954–1984*, volume 3. Edited by J. D. Faubion. Trans: Hurley, R and Others. London: Penguin Books.

Guilfoyle, M. (2008). CBT'S integration into societal networks of power. *European Journal of Psychotherapy and Counselling*. Vol. 10 (3), pp. 197–206.

Güven, E. Gökçe, G. (2018). How effective are efficiency studies?: An evaluation in the context of cognitive behavioural therapies. *Türk Psikiyatri Dergisi*. Vol. 29 (1), pp. 1–12.

Heidegger, M. (2012). *Contributions to philosophy (of the event): Of the event*. Trans: Vallega-Neu, D. Rojcewicz, R. Bloomington: Indiana University Press.

Heidegger, M. (1977). *The question concerning technology*. Trans: Lovitt. *The question concerning technology: and other essays*, pp. 3–35. New York: Harper Textbooks.

Heidegger, M. (1962). *Being and time*. Trans: John Maquarrie. London: SCM Press.

Husserl, E. (2014). *Ideas: General introduction to pure phenomenology* (1st ed.). Routledge. https://doi.org/10.4324/9780203120330

Ihde, D. (1990). *Technology and the lifeworld. The Indiana series in the philosophy of technology*. Bloomington: Indiana University Press.

Jaffa, H. V. (1952). *Thomism and Aristotelianism*. Chicago, IL: University of Chicago Press.

Kierkegaard, S. (1941). Concluding unscientific postscript. In: Friedman, M. S. (1991). (Ed.), *The worlds of existentialism: critical reader* (2nd ed. with new preface). Atlantic Highlands, NJ: Humanities Press International.

Kristeva, J. (1982). *Powers of horror. An essay on abjection*. New York: Columbia University Press.

Lévinas, E. (1967). *Totality and infinity: An essay on exteriority*. Trans: Lingis, A. Pittsburgh, PA: Duquesne University Press. (Original work published 1961).

Marshall, W. L. (2009). Manualization: A blessing or a curse? *Journal of Sexual Aggression*. Vol. 15 (2), pp. 109–120.

Miller, R. (2004). *Facing human suffering: Psychology and psychotherapy as moral engagement*. American Psychological Association. Washington, DC.

Nathan, P. (2007). Efficacy, effectiveness, and the clinical utility of psychotherapy research. In: Hofmann, S. G. Weinberger, J. (Eds,), *The art and science of psychotherapy*, pp. 69–83. New York: Routledge/Taylor & Francis Group.

Sartre, J. P. (1956). *Being and nothingness a phenomenological essay on ontology*. Citadel Press: Kensington Publishing. New York USA.

Stiegler, B. (1994). *Technics and time, 1. The fault of epimetheus*. Trans: Beardsmorth, R. Collins, G. Stanford, CA: Stanford University Press.

Verbeek, P.-P. (2016). Toward a Theory of Technological Mediation: A Program for Postphenomenological Research. In J. K. B. O. Friis, & R. P. Crease (Eds.), *Techno-science and Postphenomenology: The Manhattan Papers* (pp. 189). (Postphenomenology and Philosophy of Technology). Lexington Books.

Wampold, B. E. Baldwin, S. A. Holtforth, M. G. Imel, Z. E. (2017). What characterizes effective therapists? In: Castonguay, L. G. Hill, C. E (Eds.), *How and why are some therapists better than others? Understanding therapist effects*, pp. 37–53. American Psychological Association. Washington, DC.

Wampold, B. E. Mondin, G. W. Moody, M. Stich, E. Benson, K. Hyun-nie, A. (1997). A meta-analysis of outcome studies comparing bona fide psychotherapies: Empirically, "all must have prizes." *Psychological Bulletin*. Vol. 122, pp. 203–215.

Waller, G. Stringer, H. Mayer, C. (2012). What cognitive behavioural techniques do therapists report using when delivering cognitive behaviour therapy for the eating disorder? *Journal of Consulting and Clinical Psychology*. Vol. 80 (1), pp. 171–175.

2

FROM IMPLICATION TO APPLICATION

Introduction

> In understanding we are drawn into an event and arrive.
>
> (Gadamer)

Over recent decades, psychotherapy has undergone a significant shift towards empirically supported and evidence-based practice (EBP) in the form of manualised approaches. With strong valuative systems and outcome-driven processes, evidence-based interventions have become synonymous with government funded and 'legitimate' psychotherapeutic interventions. The result of this is that we find manualised approaches and digitalised forms of care now dominating many therapeutic settings, widening the gap between exploring the implications of theory as possibilities and the application of theory for 'evidence' (Loewenthal and Snell, 2003). But why might this be important to understand? Without drawing empirically supported models into question here; as they do exactly what they are designed to do, they attempt to take their criteria selected data and apply the findings to clinicians. What is being questioned, is the way in which we increasingly prioritise the calculable and reportable over promoting critical engagement with philosophical and ethical underpinnings in psychotherapy. Taking the view that the paradigm of empirically EBP is rooted in the demonstrable and measurable, this chapter touches on the implications faced, for idiosyncratic practices, which are rooted in a foundation of ethics and philosophy (Talens, Loewenthal and Brooks, 2025).

The landscape of many institutions which use manualised approaches often appear organised around medical and managerial models of care. NHS Talking Therapies (previously known as IAPT, 'Improving Access to Psychological Therapies'), commissioned charities, health insurance and digital mental health applications to name a few, all advertise their fidelity to EBPs and therefore an alignment with the National Institute for Health and Care Excellence (NICE). So far, this all sounds promising with clear arguments

DOI: 10.4324/9781003651666-2

that these systems have offered improved access to support and provided clear structures towards evidencing what works, it makes sense. But as we move through the chapters and look a little deeper, we start to see systemic issues emerge whilst questions of 'how' we learn, research, practise, and engage in therapy appear to take a secondary position to the metrics.

This chapter concerns itself with two different areas of orientation towards practice in psychotherapy. One position places emphasis on application by translating theory into techniques and later implementing these as predefined methods once measurement demonstrates an impact factor. The other orientation speaks to therapeutic traditions which are rooted in philosophy and ethics. For this chapter, there is a focus placed on the philosophy of hermeneutics that emphasise the importance of dialogue as a place of uncertainty from which meaning emerges and the uniqueness of each encounter. These traditions understand therapy not as an application of method to a person but as a relational practice that unfolds within a particular situation between two or more people who enter an event. There is an interest to understand how psychotherapeutic practice and research has shifted from being reflective, uncertain, and complex to increasingly being framed through a language of cost-effectiveness and outcome-driven agendas, with NICE at the very core of ensuring value for the taxpayer (https://www.nice.org.uk).

Gadamer's assertion that we are drawn into an event and arrive captures an essential essence about understanding which resists a reduction to method. Understanding, in this sense, is not something that happens to an object from a position of distance but something that happens to us as participants in an unfolding encounter. Echoes of Heidegger's 'thrownness' and 'Ereignis' (the event of appropriation) set the scene for how we are always unfolding rather than reaching an absolute conclusion. It is the divergence from Heidegger's ontological structures into the dialogical, linguistic, and historical accounts of understanding which emphasises a grounding in conversation. Here, Gadamer's insights offer a disruption to contemporary thinking in psychotherapy by demonstrating how standardising and applying conversations might in some way lose meaningful opportunities for a person. From this perspective, understanding does not subsume the other under existing frameworks but transforms through ongoing and open-ended engagement. Open ended in this sense does not mean to be in psychotherapy forever; instead, it refers to a style of conversation that has no end point or outcome in mind.

By drawing attention to the movement of implication to application, this chapter seeks to create space for reflections on how knowledge and understanding emerges within psychotherapy and explores how different kinds of practices can be supported or constrained by different types of knowing. In doing so, the chapter highlights a widening gap between exploring theory in the therapy room as a space of possibility and the application of theory which regulates the space. Taking the position that both can be helpful and unhelpful refrains from using a binary framework which thinks of manualised approaches as a 'good' or 'bad' form of therapy and moves beyond the dualistic 'for' or 'against' when exploring these models of practice. The reason for this is to move past the competitive empirical culture of comparison and instead tap into the lived experience of how different levels of application impact therapists who are at the forefront of carrying out these practices.

The chapter divides into three elements that introduce and orientate some of the key philosophies which run throughout this book. Ultimately setting the groundwork and questions which help us consider the shifting landscape towards application of psychotherapy and the complexity faced with such an endeavour.

The first element introduces key Heideggerian thinking around the concept of techné and technology. Thinking of techniques and applications as a form of technology allows us to consider how technology shapes itself over time. And by deeply looking into the philosophy of technology, how it mediates our interaction with the world. In this case, how it mediates our experience as therapists in the therapy room. The second element explores some of the key social changes such as periods of the enlightenment and how this has set the stage for the emergence of manualised practice. The final element introduces some philosophical thoughts regarding hermeneutics and the power of dialogue.

Technê of the Past and the Modern

Throughout the chapters, there is a thread which relates to Heidegger's philosophy on technology and how we have come to find ourselves in a particular relationship with it. A helpful starting point is to understand his position on the notion that modern metaphysics has used a reduced instrumental framework to interpret Aristotle too simplistically as 'means and ends'. The result of which is a distancing from a deeper philosophical Greek understanding of the way being, purpose and activity are all interconnected and together reveal an unfolding.

To understand some of Heidegger's thinking, we can look at Plato's (1967) *Protagoras* which explores the nature of virtue through a dialogue between Socrates and Protagoras himself. They are debating the notion of virtue and how this may be taught or bestowed upon others. From Socrates' perspective, whilst technical skill (technê) can be taught, wisdom cannot as he describes the case of Pericles and his sons. In return, Protagoras offers the myth of how living things came to be and the wisdom that was stolen for them. He recounts the tale of the Titan brothers, Epimetheus (afterthought/hindsight), and Prometheus (foresight/forethought), assigned by the Gods to equip mortal things with suitable powers for each kind. Epimetheus persuades his brother to allow him to distribute the powers on the condition that Prometheus review his work. On doing so, he sees that Epimetheus had failed to distribute with care and as such has left man with almost no powers. To salvage man, Prometheus steals fire from Hephaestus, and skill in the arts (a technical wisdom) from Athena in order that man can create all that is needed, including the ability for speech. The story attributes articulation and speech to the art of technê, showing the potentiality speech has as both a creative and technical endeavor. Throughout Plato's dialogues, we see notions of wisdom, virtues, and technê struggle to find clear distinctions as perspectives are not sold as objective truths. Instead, through their dialogues, technê is often portrayed as a way of bringing something into presence.

It is not until Aristotle's *Nicomachean Ethics* that we see a more centralised philosophical distinction being made between different forms of knowledge. Through the interpretations of Aristotle, we see the first restrictions and parameters placed on the concepts of technê and wisdom in a more systematic and ordered format from that of myth and dialogue. In his search, he is drawn to the idea that all behaviour is directed towards a purpose (telos). As such, teleology runs through much of Aristotle's work regarding virtue, ethics, morality, and reasoning, helping shape his conceptualisations of knowledge. Whilst Aristotle did not articulate that there were exact laws of nature, his work would be intrinsically bound with teleology. Ultimately, through Aristotle the end goal was to live well with his ethics inspiring a virtuous way.

> We deliberate not about ends but about means, for a doctor does not deliberate whether he shall heal, not an aerator whether he shall persuade, nor a statesman whether he shall produce law and order, nor does anyone else deliberate about his end. They assume the end and consider how and by what means it is to be attained....
>
> *(Aristotle,* The Nicomachean Ethics, *2004. p. 58)*

For Heidegger, interpreting this ethical framework as a reduced calculus of means and ends is potentially the reason why technê, also known as craftsmanship, would then become the application of reason to production, the purpose of which is to achieve the most effective means by which to reach a goal. This framed technê as an instrumental process, an activity involved in making and producing which promotes efficiency and mastery of a defined concept. Losing sight of notions such as poiēsis and phronesis. Poiēsis referring to a mode of bringing-forth through which something comes into presence. Not merely through human production but also through the self-emergence of natural phenomena. A process of the non-visible becoming visible is a theme we later see throughout the literature, when terms such as Weber's 'spirit', Heidegger's 'essence', and Fisher's 'atmosphere' all allude to the idea of something not quite visible behind the presence of things, but which shape how we encounter the world.

Phronesis carries a different meaning in that it is situated in the realm of practical wisdom and prudence. Phronesis requires a personal engagement and emotional investment that fully considers one's own moral action and thought regarding knowing what is best for the self and the other. The knowledge comes from a more personal and experiential engagement, where praxis is felt as an intimate and undefinable process:

> As an activity that both involved one with other people and at the same time was a realization of one's self, praxis engaged one more intimately, or afforded one less detachment, than poiesis over which one exercised an uncompromised sovereignty.
>
> *(Dunne, 1993. p. 10)*

It is technê and phronesis which have been central to the current debate in psychotherapy regarding the application of scientific knowledge versus the practitioner's practical wisdom in the therapeutic space (Smith, 2009; Falkum, 2008). It is the ways in which these forms of knowledge posit a different relationship towards means and ends. This can at times be seen through the science-practice gap, which is rooted in polarised standpoints regarding a standardised working practice versus an autonomous practice shaped by the encounter. The move towards a more technical understanding of the world which privileges 'Theoria' over 'Praxis' can become problematic when there is an overreliance on technical knowledge. The use of tools and theory as an approach to encounter and engage with people can overlook the significant need to form a practice from a more embodied source of knowledge (Smeeton, 2017).

Rationality of the Enlightenment

If Aristotle was to give us an account of human flourishing through the pursuit of the 'good life' then the 'Enlightenment' would surely provide us with the tools; we need to carry out such a task. In the 17th and 18th centuries, Europe would undergo a transformation of ideas which would revolutionise the ways in which society functions. Known as the 'Age of reason' it formed part of an intellectual and philosophical movement that would see reason and science become the dominant force for progress. Rationalism would offer a way in which to obtain knowledge alongside evidence of the senses, whilst faith and tradition would struggle to maintain authority in the same manner.

Here we encounter the core principles and notion of modernity, that of the individual, scientific truth, freedom, and social progress on a scale never witnessed before (Cahoone, 2010). A sentiment which was captured so poignantly by Friedrich Nietzsche's 'The Madman' in which his character arrives in the town square perhaps too early for people to recognise his cries of "*God is dead. God remains dead. And we have killed him*" (Nietzsche, 1974. p. 181). He illustrates the death of a belief system which underpins a foundational meaning, and certainty for many. There is a recognition that the door is open both to opportunity and to a fear of a potential nihilism and disengagement as 'meaning' is no longer defined but instead sits in flux. Nietzsche encourages that everyone takes up their uniqueness and forges their own meaning in a world of chaos whilst observing a constant attempt to create universal foundations stating: "every philosopher so far: *as soon as they approached the study of morality: they wanted to supply a rational foundation for morality – and every philosopher so far believes that he has provided such a foundation*" (Nietzsche, 1966. p. 98).

This observation gives a sense of a society which has started ordering, putting together, and developing fixed understanding from a rational perspective. A blueprint is being created for how society conducts itself based on and steered towards rationality as the new authority. His predictions and fears of future thought becoming uniformed and homogenous might be contrasted with manualised approaches which are increasingly rooted in rationality and uniformed parameters. The progressive nature of rationality evoked a counter-enlightenment movement which took on its own anti-rationalist standpoint as the societal and cultural implications of these shifts in thought were taking hold. Theodor Adorno and Max Horkheimer (1997) would go about developing one of the most critical challenges to tackle the issues of the 'Enlightenment', highlighting the core problems faced with what they called a mass deception and the administrative culture it had produced: "*Culture as a common denominator already contains in embryo that schematization and process of cataloguing and classification which bring culture within the sphere of administration*" (Adorno and Horkheimer, 1997. p. 131).

These philosophical assumptions are ever present in today's psychotherapy and form a large part of disagreement towards the ways we validate empirically supported therapies (Norcross et al., 2005), the basis of which sits with the idea of underlying mechanisms which are causal to the phenomenon in question. This led to the creation of systems and laws which are observable in format and verifiable through experiments. Psychology as a discipline would adopt this framework of knowledge to produce a scientific approach to the individual. Sigmund Freud would go on to develop what his editors termed 'Project for a Scientific Psychology' in which his opening remarks are:

> The intention is to furnish a psychology that shall be a natural science: its aim, that is, is to represent physical processes as quantitatively determined

stats of specifiable material particles and so to make them plain and void of contradictions.

(Freud, 1995. p. 87)

It would become only a matter of time before we would begin to apply this science to ourselves and potentially create what Freud (1995) described as a science of the soul. After all, if science has worked so well for objects and bodies, why not the human mind also? It opens the question of Freud attempting to engage with the times in a way that would be taken seriously. Afterall, science would need some convincing before it would open the gates to people it had previously regarded as charlatans, and so the calculable and visible would become essential to evidence its status. Simultaneously, during the same period, technology is shifting its very definition. We see the expansion from a rational and applicable knowledge, which translates itself into a material tool with a specific purpose, to a technology that now *does* through systems of thinking such as methodologies, education, ideas, and process (Carroll, 2017).

The Emergence of Manualised Practice

The emergence of manualised practice can be rooted in the domain of behavioural science which is described as an "offspring of the marriage of a philosophy and a technique" (Ehrenwald, 1991. p. 445). Whilst manualised practice is not specific to any one branch of psychotherapy, we can instead illuminate the core characteristics of which it lends itself. We can take a current strand of manualised practice such as cognitive behavioural therapy (CBT) and trace its roots to demonstrate some central components.

Based on a causal-reductive and materialistic view of the human condition, behavioural psychologists viewed human action as dependent on the consequences of any previous actions. Meanwhile, cognitive theories were rooted in the philosophical underpinnings of Stoic logic (Beck, 1979). With the combination of logic and behaviour laying the foundations, CBT's visible aspects lend themselves to empirical measurements and, as such, sit comfortably within the paradigm of EBP. Where Randomised Controlled Trials (RCTs) can be deployed to evaluate effectiveness of interventions. The primary purpose of RCT is the integration between sciences, patient preference, and clinical expertise as a model for practice (Cochrane, 1972). Centred on the notions of scientific research and evidence, EBP is situated within a debate between subjective experience of practice and the objective interpretation of science (Falkum, 2008). In a later chapter we will explore in more depth where the expertise element of RCTs is potentially failing when it comes to research.

Therapies such as CBT offer an established collection of empirically based interventions which are tested, outcome measured, and repeatable on a large scale (Beck, 2011). Encompassing a collaborative process, CBT offers the practitioner and client a set of skills and techniques for changes being sought (Dobson, 2010). Designed as a pragmatic approach, CBT is the combination of behavioural psychology merged with theories of cognition (Mahoney, 1995). Its templates and manuals of treatment have expanded across a wide range of diagnostic matters and are considered "an active, problem focused approach to treatment" (Dobson, 2010. p. 43). In essence, CBT responds to a problem with the best empirically tested set of tools available, highlighting the way logic, objective knowledge, the visible and knowable treat technique as a tool 'ready-to-hand' to achieve its goals. This is a long way off from existential thought, which is described as "the reaction against the static, the abstract, the purely rational, the merely irrational, in favour of the dynamic" (Friedman, 1991. pp. 3–4).

Currently, the landscape of contemporary psychotherapy appears to be marked by a restrictive idea that there is an inherent 'goal' of symptom reduction whilst the ways to attain such a goal have exponentially grown and diversified. In effect, finding the most efficient ways to achieve this has in turn become its own goal (Dunne, 1993). Approaches increasingly concern themselves with ideas of 'efficiency' and repeatable 'manualised methods' which have their own tailored formats to produce knowledge, often in the form of RCT's (Dalal, 2018. Dobson, 2010. Wampold et al., 2017. Waller, Stringer and Meyer, 2012). This is both valuable and problematic when large quantities of the same format and specification start to present as a given universal 'truth' based on 'evidence' rather than a truth which has derived from the repeated nature of the parameters set. If you offer a choice of three answers to a question, you can only have three possible outcomes, the results will present as 'evidence' towards a 'truth', but it would always be a perpetual subset of a larger 'truth' in essence. There is an argument to be made that this is less to do with science and more to do with a calculative industry. For Heaton (2014) there is a scientism which takes place when there are claims of one reality. He highlights how scientism "*misunderstands science. Good scientists are well aware that there are many ways of understanding reality*" (p. 34).

The central focus of EBP is on establishing the efficacy of a given technique for the purpose of quantifiable dimensions. This, however, has been the subject of critique, prompting concern towards the reductive nature which fails to incorporate the complexities of the self as a whole and negate the therapeutic relationship (Elkins, 2017). Research within CBT predominantly reflects on effectiveness by measuring impact factors on the reduction of symptoms relating to a diagnosis. What is less evident is research that can meaningfully evaluate the relationship technique has with the therapist and their practice (Wampold et al., 2017). This is of relevance as there is an indication that the therapeutic alliance accounted for a 21% variance on outcomes in psychotherapy, whereas different interventions accounted for a 2% variance on outcomes (Wampold, 2001). This is what is known as the 'therapist effect' in which studies show that the relationship between therapist and clients is the biggest determinant for change (Johns et al., 2018).

For this reason, there is a greater call for a move from an empirically based understanding to practice-based evidence which is explored further in the literature when considering the practice gap which emerges in psychotherapy. There is a sense that manualised interventions can detract from a practice-based understanding of psychotherapy and as such "*manuals focus attention toward a wasteland and away from fertile ground*" (Wampold, 2001. p. 212). This in essence forces the issue and highlights how evidence-based treatments and research depend on an empirically reduced conceptualisation of psychotherapy (Berg and Slaattelid, 2017). This is not to say that practice-based evidence does not enter a calculus as there are numerous examples of attempts to quantify and measure practice and the therapeutic relationship. Several examples include research into 'effective' therapist characteristics (Wampold et al., 2017) which has improved previous claims that the therapist was a neglected variable in psychotherapy research and reinforced by the rise of manual effectiveness (Garfield, 1997). The 'real relationship inventory' which is measured against a 24-item scale with the two subscales of realism and genuineness to elicit a score is also an example of quantitative measures (Gelso, Kelley and Fuertes, 2005). However, some researchers interpret these findings through a contextual model rather than a medical model, arguing that psychotherapy provides a framework for discovery, disputing the notion that its benefits derive from any single ingredient of an intervention (Wampold et al., 2017).

As previously addressed, we consider how manualised practices and research are increasingly aligned with a calculative industry, which is potentially motivated by good numbers rather than good science. But does this have the potential to create a form of scientism when metrics devoid of context are utilised as 'evidence' to paint a picture of reality.

Fusion of Horizons as Endless Possibility

So far, we have seen how some of the social conditions and developments in technological thinking have offered fertile ground for the application of thought to become central to progress and shape the world. In relation to therapeutic practice, might our use of theories to know about the other draw us into treating interpretation as a closed end point of knowing rather than letting emerging experience in an encounter become its own valid knowledge system.

Hans-Georg Gadamer's (2000) '*fusion of horizons*' helps us see how conversations have an ability to infuse when there is an 'openness' available. That with technology as is with conversation, there is a hermeneutic element towards notions of 'truth' and discovery (Mitcham, 1978). This takes up the position that knowledge is fluid and that whilst metric outcomes play a role in developing understanding, they are part of the picture rather than the whole picture. Within psychotherapy there is a call for a practice-centred critique towards psychotherapy when considering manualised approaches such as CBT (Stewart-sicking, 2015). There are concerns regarding how training, standardisation, professionalisation, and digitalisation monopolise the psychotherapeutic space, which at its core holds the therapeutic relationship as its most valued asset and often as a prerequisite for therapy. We can see how the philosophy of hermeneutics and conversation are paramount to learning and development. How a fusion of ideas and words help us to diversify our own thinking and experiences as a process rather than an end goal (Gadamer, 2000). Thus, therapy can be seen as an experientially based process of education towards a sense of fully becoming (Satir, 1982).

This involves a shift from the ordered and understandable towards ideas and a language which attempts to speak in a way that is beyond categorisations and binary concepts. Beyond in the sense that it can become messy and entangled in uncertainty as we move away from defined objects which lend themselves to measurement and analysis as a singular and towards unexplored territories and concepts which are relational and fluid. The importance of this is that we are given capacity to create, redefine, and evolve if offered a language from which to build a new house of being (Heidegger, 2012). It is a language which departs from its roots within a system of knowledge and a system of labelling and categorising that can flourish.

Hermeneutics and understanding in this sense can be seen as an adventure through its uncertainty, offering a multiplicity of meaning. Through lending ourselves to a fluid and unrestrictive hermeneutical encounter, we can broaden the horizon of self-knowledge and human experience (Gadamer, 1989). Central to the idea of expanding horizons is the notion that conversation requires a form of 'openness' within language and positions itself as an unfinished event. This shows how the ongoing nature of discourse offers a foundation of potentiality when dialogue is not restricted or pre-established. There is a call to hold space that is not defined and that can move through tensions, complexities, and paradoxes in psychotherapeutic practice. This is not in the name of obscurantism but rather a giving room for what might emerge as opposed to seeking 'evidence' to reaffirm a status quo. Allowing ourselves as practitioners and researchers to tolerate 'being adrift' (Ogden, 1997) could be helpful in connecting to situations with a deeper level of complexity and creativity. As such, the ethics of the 'Other' are considered in relation to the tension held between 'self' and being a 'therapist' which emerges as a complex world to navigate.

For Gadamer as is for Heidegger, language is regarded as the '*house of being*' from which understanding is both created and achieved. In this sense, language is linked to a 'happening' (Geschehen) or emerging event which positions language as a form of 'becoming' (Vandevelde, 2014). Whilst there can be pre-established meaning, language also can create and emerge as a unique moment for and from an individual. From this perspective, we are always part of the language from which we speak. The implication of this for psychotherapy can be seen as the need to hold space for both new and already established knowledge. However, to lend oneself to such an endeavour, the therapist must be able to take up the position of '*not knowing*'. Just as a continuous testing of hypothesis is a hermeneutic interpretation, in and of itself, the therapy room too becomes a continual loop of investigation and experimentation with its hypothesis for meaning and understanding to emerge. This asks how we might move from pre-established methods of analysis rooted in a defined language to a conversation about inclusion and renewal of the personal (Bida, 2018). Taking on Heidegger's (2012) concept of language, in particular, poetic language can be considered as a form of dwelling. Whilst language and meaning are to some degree inherited, we are always in some way part of the language from which we speak as it speaks us into '*being*'. This identifies the need for psychotherapy to hold space for a renewed sense of self through speech, articulating how "*... the role of the therapist is that of a conversational artist – an architect of the dialogical process – whose expertise is in the arena of creating space for and facilitating a dialogical conversation*" (Anderson and Goolishian, 1992. p. 27). This delves into the impact on therapy sessions, when there is little to no space offered outside the agenda of manualised practices and institutions which aim for high levels of 'efficacy'.

Rather than producing or replicating knowledge, can psychotherapy become a space that hears the *unfolding which takes place?* What stands out is the way in which this resists the reduction of experience into method or measure. It recognises that both therapist and client participate in the unfolding of meaning and that such meaning is always situated, relational, and in motion. We are therefore encouraged to consider holding conversations with the tension of uncertainty. In holding back from entering application and method we lend ourselves to an '*openess*' and a '*fusion of horizons*' (Gadamer, 2000) helps us see how conversations have an ability to infuse when and where we find ourselves changed in some way by what is being encountered with the other. It can be argued that being influenced by emerging context is paramount to therapy in the form of responsiveness and adapting to clients (Watson and Wiseman, 2024). This takes up the position that knowledge is fluid and that whilst metric outcomes play a role in developing understanding, they are part of the picture rather than the whole picture.

What then, of a therapeutic practice that produces and applies repeatable methods in the name of outcome rather than authentic engagement? A practice that no longer speaks to us about us but instead becomes a tool at our disposal. It would be an error and a narrow thinking to assume that the '*effectiveness*' of psychotherapy can be understood simply from symptom reduction. With consensus across most therapeutic approaches that the therapeutic relationship accounts for a greater impact on outcomes than specific techniques and interventions used in therapy rooms (Narcross and Lambert, 2018), there are clearly other ways to understand what matters. As such, there is a call for research which orientates towards understanding the role of technical and relational aspects of therapy (Wampold, 2001). Understanding how this relationship is mediated by technique and method sits as a central question within this book.

Essentially, a question is developing about the role that different forms of knowledge play in our understanding of a given situation. It explores if we can move towards a way of being that opens possibility rather than the demand to know concretely which can become technical and procedural in nature, thereby distancing the personal and ontological from creative ownership. Research and psychotherapy are laden with method and tools so much that they attempt to produce a 'goal'. This is not considered problematic in the sense that it too is potentially inescapable. Instead, what is highlight is an ethical awareness of how the demand to know the '*Other*' and categorise them is potentially in service to social, economic, and political systems rather than offering reflection.

Further considering the ethical, we can begin with Lévinas because it is the active failure of the task to understand or comprehend the '*Other*' which sits as an ethical position. So rather than taking up a starting point from which to order and make a coherent argument, instead it is about taking up an exploratory nature and allowing a conversation to emerge from different locations, but which are interconnected and indebted to each other. Gilles Deleuze and Felix Guattari's (2004) post-structural concept of the rhizome best articulates how this might be thought about and considered. Their work alludes to a network of thought which can be nonlinear, non-hierarchical, and with no designed order or coherency, which allows for connections, entry, and exit points in any given moment. This liberates one from a traditional path of knowledge as there is no origin or genesis and can be without a beginning, middle, or end. Within this, there are characteristics which are assigned to the rhizome which feel relevant for the current conversation. Firstly, the principle of connection in which any connection can be made and must be made, a trait one might associate with Freud's (1995) 'free association' or phenomenology's 'horizontalization' in which we put aside the hieratical value systems and allow space for the other to move freely within their own interpretation. This is explored through calculative and meditative (sober) thinking in which one's ability to meander off course and take up a different experience is of importance for the ways we are shaped (Heidegger, 1959. Wrathall, 2019).

Secondly, the principle of multiplicity and the idea that "Multiplicities are rhizomatic, and expose arborescent pseudo-multiplicities for what they are" (Deleuze and Guattari, 2004. p. 7), a concept which lends itself to the plurality of appearances to the plurality of appearances but which remain subordinate to an underlying structure.

Thirdly, rupture and the lines that tie back together from which the rhizomes can emerge once again. The significance of which is to show that we can never be separated despite the illusion that we are and here "is why one can never posit a dualism or a dichotomy, even in the rudimentary form of the good and the bad" (Deleuze and Guattari, 2004. p. 9). As we have seen through the chapter, there is a drive to overcome and to transcend the entanglement we encounter with the hermeneutic challenge, in which we try to make sense of and resolve the complexity of us and the world. Thinking that in some way this can be achieved through method, whether by suspending, forgetting, bracketing, or simply ignoring to capture and make knowable. In this sense, the increased take-up of method becomes a way of avoiding the uncertainty we sit with.

References

Adorno, T. Horkheimer, M. (1997). *Dialectic of enlightenment.* Trans: Cumming, J. New York: Verso.

Anderson, H. Goolishian, H. (1992). The client is the expert: A not-knowing approach to therapy. In: McNamee, S. Gergen, K. J. (Eds.), *Therapy as social construction,* pp. 25–39. Sage Publications, Inc. Newbury Park, CA

Aristotle. (2004). *The Nicomachean ethics.* Trans: Thomson, J. A. K. London: Penguin Books.

Beck, A. T. (1979). *Cognitive therapy of depression.* New York: Guilford Press.

Beck, J. S. (2011). *Cognitive behaviour therapy: Basics and beyond* (2nd ed.). New York: Guilford Press.

Berg, H. Slaattelid, R. (2017). Facts and values in psychotherapy: A critique of the empirical reduction of psychotherapy within evidence-based practice. *Journal of Evaluation in Clinical Practice.* Vol. 23, 1075–1080.

Bida, A. (2018). Heidegger and 'dwelling'. In: *Mapping home in contemporary narratives, geocriticism and spatial literary studies*. Cham: Palgrave Macmillan. https://doi.org/10.1007/978-3-319-97967-0_2

Brown, J. Dreis, S. Nace, D. K. (1999). What really makes a difference in psychotherapy outcome? Why does managed care want to know? In: Hubble, M. A. Duncan, B. L. Miller, S. D. (Eds.), *The heart and soul of change: What works in therapy*, pp. 389–406. Washington, DC: American Psychological Association.

Cahoone, L. (2010). *The modern intellectual tradition: From Descartes to Derrida. Course guidebook*. The Great Courses. Chantilly, VA

Carroll, L. S. L. (2017). A comprehensive definition of technology from an ethological perspective. *Social Sciences*. Vol. 6 (4), pp. 1–20. https://doi.org/10.3390/socsci6040126

Cochrane, A. L. (1972). *Effectiveness and Efficiency: Random Reflections on Health Services*. London: Nuffield Provincial Hospitals Trust.

Dalal, F. (2018). *CBT: The cognitive behavioural tsunami. Managerialism, politics and the corruptions of science*. New York: Routledge.

Deleuze, G. Guattari, F. (2004). *A thousand plateaus*. New York: Continuum.

Dobson, K. S. (2010). *Handbook of cognitive behavioural therapies* (3rd ed.). New York: The Guildford Press.

Dunne, J. (1993). *Back to the rough ground: Practical judgment and the Lure of Technique*. IN: University of Notre Dame. Indiana, USA

Ehrenwald, J. (1991). *The history of psychotherapy*. London: Jason Aronson Inc.

Elkins, D. (2017). The medical model in psychotherapy. Its limitations and failures. *Journal of Humanistic Psychology*. Vol. 49 (1), pp. 66–84.

Falkum, E. (2008). Phronesis and Techne: The debate on evidence-based medicine in psychiatry and psychotherapy. *Philosophy, Psychiatry and Psychology*. Vol. 15 (2), pp. 141–149.

Freud, S. (1995). *The Freud Reader edited by Peter Gay*. London: Vintage Originals.

Friedman, M. S. (1991). *The worlds of existentialism: Critical reader* (2nd ed. with new preface). Atlantic Highlands, NJ: Humanities Press International.

Gadamer, H. G. (2000). *Truth and method*. Trans: Weinsheimer, J. Marshall, D. G. New York: Continuum.

Gadamer, H. G. (1989). Back from Syracuse? Trans: McCumber, J. *Critical Inquiry*. Vol. 15 (2), pp. 427–430.

Garfield, L. (1997). The therapist as a neglected variable in psychotherapy research. *Clinical Psychology – Science and Practice*. Vol. 4, pp. 40–43.

Gelso, C. J. Kelley, F. A. Fuertes, J. N. (2005). Measuring the real relationship in psychotherapy: Initial validation of the therapist form. *Journal of Counseling Psychology*. Vol. 52 (4), pp. 640–649.

Heaton, J. M. (2014). *Wittgenstein and psychotherapy. From paradox to wonder*. Palgrave Macmillan UK. London, England.

Heidegger, M. (2012). *Contributions to philosophy (of the event): Of the event*. Trans: Vallega-Neu, D. Rojcewicz, R. Bloomington: Indiana University Press.

Heidegger, M. (1959). *Discourse on thinking*. Trans: Anderson, J. M. Freund, H. E. New York: Harper & Row.

Johns, R. G. Barkham, M. Kellett, S. Saxon, D. (2018). A systematic review of therapist effects: A critical narrative update and refinement to review. *Clinical Psychology Review*. Vol. 67, pp. 78–93. https://doi.org/10.1016/j.cpr.2018.08.004

Loewenthal, D. Snell, R. (2003). *Post-modernism for psychotherapists a critical reader*. East Sussex: Routledge. Hove, East Sussex

Mahoney, M. J. (1995). Theoretical developments in the cognitive and constructive psychotherapies. In: *Cognitive and constructive psychotherapies: Recent developments in theory, research, and practice*. New York: Springer. Ed. Mahoney, M. J, pp. 3–24.

Mitcham, C. (1978). Types of technology. *Research in Philosophy and Technology*. Vol. 1, pp. 229–294.

Narcross, J. Lambert, M. (2018). Psychotherapy relationships that work III. *Journal of Psychotherapy*. Vol. 5, pp. 303–315.

Nietzsche, F. (1974). *The Gay Science with a prelude in rhymes and an appendix of songs*. Trans: Kaufman, W. New York: Vintage Books.

Nietzsche, F. (1966). *Beyond good and evil. Prelude to a philosophy of the future*. Trans: Kaufmann, W. Random House Inc. New York, NY

Norcross, J. Levant, R. Beutler, L. (2005). *Evidence-based practices in mental health: Debate and dialogue on the fundamental questions*. Washington, DC: American Psychological Association Press.

Ogden, T. (1997). Reverie and interpretation. *The Psychoanalytic Quarterly*. Vol. 66, pp. 567–595.

Plato. (1967). *Plato in twelve volumes,* Vol 3. Trans: Lamb, W. R. M. Cambridge, MA: Harvard University Press and London: William Heinemann Ltd.

Satir, V. (1982). The therapist and family therapy: Process model. In A. Horne and M. Ohlsen (Eds.), *Family counselling and therapy*. Itasca, IL: Peacock Publications.

Smeeton, J. (2017). From Aristotle to Arendt: A phenomenological exploration of forms of knowledge and practice in the context of child protection social work in the UK. *Qualitative Social Work*. Vol. 16 (1), pp. 14–28.

Smith, K. R. (2009). Psychotherapy as applied science or moral praxis: The limitations of empirically supported treatment. *Journal of Theoretical and Philosophical Psychology*. Vol. 29 (1), pp. 34–46.

Stewart-sicking, J. (2015). Cognitive therapy and the punctual self: Using an ascetical framework to critique approaches to psychotherapy. *Pastoral Psychology*. Vol. 64 (1). https://doi.org/10.1007/s11089-013-0588-7

Talens, P. Loewenthal, D. Brooks, O. (2025). Psychotherapeutic research and practice: Do we need to talk about 'efficacy'? In: *Developing psychotherapeutic innovation and imagination through phenomenology and qualitative research*. London: Routledge. Ed. Loewenthal, D and Abela, A. pp. 220–234

Vandevelde, P. (2014). Language as the house of being? How to bring intelligibility to Heidegger while keeping the excitement. *Philosophy Compass*. Vol. 9, pp. 253–262. https://doi.org/10.1111/phc3.12117

Waller, G. Stringer, H. Mayer, C. (2012). What cognitive behavioural techniques do therapists report using when delivering cognitive behaviour therapy for the eating disorder? *Journal of Consulting and Clinical Psychology*. Vol. 80 (1), pp. 171–175.

Wampold, B. E. (2001). *The great psychotherapy debate: Models, methods, and findings*. Mahwah, NJ: Erlbaum.

Wampold, B. E., Baldwin, S. A., Holtforth, M. G. Imel, Z. E. (2017). What characterizes effective therapists? In: Castonguay, L. G. Hill, C. E (Eds.), *How and why are some therapists better than others? Understanding therapist effects*, pp. 37–53. American Psychological Association. Washington, DC

Wampold, B. E. Mondin, G. W. Moody, M. Stich, E. Benson, K. Hyun-nie, A. (1997). A meta-analysis of outcome studies comparing bona fide psychotherapies: Empirically, "all must have prizes." *Psychological Bulletin*. Vol. 122, pp. 203–215.

Watson, J. C. Wiseman, H. (2024). Responsiveness: Can psychotherapies and psychotherapists adapt effectively to participant and clinical contexts? In: Leong, F. T. L. Callahan, J. L. Zimmerman, J. Constantino, J. M. Eubanks, C. F. (Eds.), *APA handbook of psychotherapy: Evidence-based practice, practice-based evidence, and contextual participant-driven practice*, pp. 95–115. American Psychological Association. https://doi.org/10.1037/0000354-007

Wrathall, M. (2019). The task of thinking in a technological age. In: Wendland, A. J. Merwin, C. Hadjioannou, C. (Eds.), *Heidegger on technology*. New York: Routledge. www.nice.org.uk

3

FROM THEORY TO CALCULATION

Introduction

> Could it think, the heart would stop beating.
>
> (Fernando Pessoa)

Psychotherapy is concerned with experience, and from a phenomenological frame, allowing the meaning and understanding of that experience emerge over time and in context. As discussed in the previous chapter, this can closely align with a 'bringing-forth' (poiēsis) and technê as a practice of crafting with emerging experience, the process and outcome of which can be a form of revealing. A diagnostic model may be concerned with ordering and categorising specific experiences geared towards developing interventions. Aligned with 'challenging-forth' and 'enframing', this form of practice controls all aspects of the process including the craftsman in a way of being and ordering the environment into a particular reality. This is a reality in which efficiency is a dominant value and the world becomes interpreted through usefulness and control, often at the cost of poetic and contemplative ways of seeing.

The drive to calculate which interventions are most 'effective' has become ever more important as empirically supported, and cost-effective approaches are utilised by funding bodies. This cultural shift towards a calculative and measurable sense of people's experience draws a concern in relation to its business-like and systematising application of psychotherapy. The economy of supply and demand raises implications for psychotherapy when there is a pressure to regulate, manage, steer, and upscale therapeutic support to the masses (Jackson and Rizq, 2019). Manualised approaches become subject to a form of 'governing by numbers' within the industry, setting up and reinforcing a political power derived from the calculative practices in place (Porter, 1996; Miller, 2001).

The embedded structures towards research and practice faces further problems when outcome measures fail to articulate or respond to the complex,

DOI: 10.4324/9781003651666-3

multi-layered, unmapped, and unmeasurable aspects of psychotherapy. It raises a question regarding the nature of knowledge and the ethical stance taken within psychotherapy (Miller, 2004). This highlights a different kind of cost when practice is primarily shaped by measurement and application. What might be lost in practice and research when uncertainty and attentiveness is bypassed for repeatability, efficiency, and measurable outcomes? This is not an argument against the idea of measurements or systems, all of which have their value and place in the world of psychotherapy. What is being asked here is, why are we increasingly drawn towards a practice in which method and technique being applied from the outset appear valued over practice which articulates the uniqueness of each encounter?

The following chapter explores three points of interest to help consider some of these questions and to offer thought in relation to how this position has come about. The first point considers how the medical model with all its economic and political ties offers an already existing infrastructure for calculative modes of practice. The second point focuses on Mark Fisher's concept of 'capitalist realism' and the atmospheric background as the constant framing from which professional practices emerge already entangled with economy and efficiency. Finally, maintaining the theme of philosophical underpinnings towards technology, Heideggerian notions of '*enframing*' and '*indebtedness*' open the conversation towards our use of technology. By exploring psychotherapy as a cultural practice (Loewenthal, 2020), we begin to see how therapy is used more directly as a tool within a service industry rather than an unfolding encounter.

Conforming to Infrastructure

In the previous chapter, we saw how culture and theory in psychotherapy began to merge into more observational and measurable practices. Here in the United Kingdom, we have seen manualised practice exponentially increase and become an ever more integrated part of the therapeutic endeavour. Manualised interventions such as cognitive behavioural therapy (CBT) have undergone rapid expansion and implementation in the last few decades. Endorsement from the 'National Institute for Health and Care Excellence' (NICE) has seen CBT become a political favourite and rolled out as a front-line provision for the 'National Health Service' (NHS). This provision has become one of the most adopted treatments in adults (Dobson, 2010) and a dominant force both within the therapeutic field and across multiple institutions (Dalal, 2018). Encountered as an observable, and measurable approach to understanding human behaviour and process of change, CBT lends itself to a scientific and calculable rationale (Fishman, Rego and Muller, 2011). As such, there is a strong empirical evidence base for CBT and other manualised practices. However, we also know there is no empirical support for the idea that manualised interventions are more effective than interventions which are non-manualised, making the case that they should not be promoted as advanced or clinically superior (Truijens, Zühlke-van Hulzen and Vanheule, 2019; King and Moutsou, 2010). Therefore, if the science isn't there (Shedler, 2018), what then, might we understand from this exponential rise?

Could it be the case that some external systems work and regulate better with each other? And so, the widespread recognition may also be influenced by compatibility and comfortable integration with social networks of power. With calculative and repeatable manuals lending themselves to already existing infrastructures built for the medical model, they can be distributed under cost-effective and time-efficient policies, becoming a politically convenient form of technology (Guilfoyle, 2008).

This has been most visible through the development of the governmental scheme NHS Talking Therapies (previously known as 'Improving Access to Psychological Therapies', IAPT), which was designed to address the economic, social, and individual cost of mental health in the United Kingdom. The scheme was created by Richard Layard, an economist, and David Clarke, a leading expert in CBT, with the intention to deliver better mental health support on an unprecedented scale. By working the scheme into the blueprint of the medical model, it would ensure that therapeutic interventions would be delivered with the same rigour as any other medical intervention.

To achieve this rigour, RCTs would be an essential method of enquiry for psychotherapy which steers away from traditional models of research (Layard and Clarke, 2014). With empirical evidence, integrity of treatment, and value for money as the goal, efficiency becomes central to the endeavour despite it not being a satisfactory model of psychotherapy (Goldfried and Eubanks-Carter, 2004). What has emerged is an evidence-based race where production of outcome is politically and economically motivated (Jackson and Rizq, 2019; Guilfoyle, 2008). The concern being that other analytic, existential, and phenomenological frameworks may be forced into this race to stay relevant, pushing modalities to transform into more formulaic and simplified versions and becoming uprooted from their philosophical grounding. Overtime, this leads to the development of increasingly condensed versions which fit reduced parameters and ways of practice. The implications of this can already be seen within the history of CBT and the emergence of its 'third wave'. This wave is attempting to counter CBT's previous shift from structural self-knowledge to functional process (Ruggiero et al., 2018) by incorporating models of acceptance, mindfulness, and meaning to bring back a level of attunment (Haddock, 2022).

There is consensus across various psychotherapeutic approaches articulating the therapeutic relationship to be at the core of psychotherapy (Narcross and Lambert, 2018). This highlights the risk of doing more harm than good if we fail to consider a wider scope beyond the metric measures (Orange, 2011). What is being addressed is a fundamental concern regarding the way metrics and efficiency are becoming the principal form of enquiry over a framework that seeks to be discovery-oriented and explores wider contextual understanding of psychotherapy. Frameworks in research and practice which offer opportunities beyond the usual methodologies. It is this dilemma which has brought this book to consider the ways in which manualised encounters shape the experience of the therapist and their clients. Do these practices obscure or restrict therapists being with their clients in some way?

As the infrastructure of calculative mechanisms develops, we see ever more score sheets and quantitative results in the name of research becoming targets and measurements of success (Shore and Wright, 2024). With institutions such as 'NHS Talking Therapies' having monitoring systems and minimum data sets built into their very fabric, how does this shape the therapeutic encounter? Furthermore, we see screening tools such as 'Patient Health care Questionnaire' (PHQ-9), the 'Anxiety Disorder Assessment' (GAD-7), and sessional CORE forms provide a constant stream of evaluation and a priority for the ordering of provision. The implication of which is that this widespread system of bureaucratic screening and monitoring becomes second nature for the people who use the service (Bendall and McGrath, 2020). The implication for research and evidence is that the screening tools are not purely to order provision. They gather data from an already established set of interventions, freezing out other practices under the guise that they are not empirically supported. These data are later used as the evidence for clinicians to select the best model of practice and as such become a self-reinforcing and self-evidencing feedback loop. But could we move the conversation beyond our usual practical use of technique and intervention as a technology of change? Instead, start to consider the implications for the therapist and client when conversations are systematised to yield outcomes and maximise metric results.

Therapies as technologies are well documented and have a long history of providing help to overcome difficult situations in life (Kasavina, 2017. p. 75). Seen as an applied science or technology of change, 'Empirically Supported Treatments' (ESTs) engage in a moral praxis, with "its own view of the good, while not acknowledging that it is doing so" (Smith et al., 2009. p. 40). And whilst technique has always been an established part of therapy, whether in the form of a modality or a cultural practice (Fonagy, Roth and Higgitt, 2005; Gross, 1978), the emergence of EST has seen an increasing consensus of therapy as a form of technics and applied science. One in which therapists respond in some way to knowledge that has been acquired predominantly through research and training (Parker, 2002). Considered as a response to a hyper-rational understanding of 'efficiency' (Dalal,

2018), CBT with other manualised and technological approaches are increasingly being linked to a culture of neoliberalism which is concerned with specialisation and industrialisation through its applications (Jackson and Rizq, 2019). This becomes problematic when therapeutic practice and research is repeatedly carried out through a technical lens, as it can become the only medium by which the world shows up for the therapist and researcher in return.

Capitalism and Efficiency

Having lightly touched upon evolutions of psychotherapy in relation to method integrating with pre-existing structures, we now look at the ways in which epistemologies and cultural thought have merged into modern-day manualised practices. Of particular interest is to draw on Max Weber's (2001) understanding of the Protestant ethic and his concept of the 'Iron Cage'. The purpose of which is to help illuminate some of the tensions that emerge within a society or industry that labels itself as progressive whilst remaining deeply chained and structured by rationalising forces no matter the cost. In his work *The Protestant Ethic and the Spirit of Capitalism*, Weber examines how shifts in religious thought have helped give rise to new form of economic ethos. He traces how the Calvinist doctrine of predestination generated a drive towards disciplined labour, and that worldly success functioned as a reassurance to be among the elect. Psychologically, this offered a way to cope with existential uncertainty about salvation, as calculable and measurable achievements became symbols of self-discipline and a rational conduct, showing dedication. It could be argued that with salvation hidden and only known to God, people would turn to more visible and calculable ways of engaging with the world through orderly life, and discipline. His idea of disenchantment with the world refers to the process by which the world becomes understood and explainable, moving away from mystery and the ineffable. A dynamic which resonates with today's tendencies to quantify mental health through progress and demonstrative outcomes, all of which play a role in an evaluative culture not too dissimilar from earlier moral frameworks.

To bring Weber's work into contemporary day, one can explore Mark Fisher's (2009) notion of 'capitalist realism' as a framework for understanding how these rationalising tendencies are not only institutional but also psychological. Capitalist realism describes the pervasive nature of capitalism not simply as a dominant economic system but as the only conceivable system from which all else emerges, including culture and subjectivity. This sets the scene that practices such as psychotherapy are always at risk of being orientated towards optimisation within this environment as no other options feel viable. It is an all-encompassing ideology that shapes the way we think and act in the world. One in which there is a lack of space afforded to questions about the conditions themselves, making any challenge to the system ineffective. Eventually the system becomes so enclosed and bound by practices and bureaucracy that other possibilities become outcast and devalued.

Here too Weber was attentive to the way ideals from the Enlightenment contributed to increasingly efficient systems that risk enclosing individuals within structures that favour instrumental reasoning. Indeed, Weber feared that there would be problems posed with such a take-up of application in society. He argued that the application of science serves to break down societies into their component parts rather than seeing them as a connected whole, making everything as efficient as possible and offering more detailed examinations of constituted parts. He was conscious not only to the emergence of modern rationality but also to the unintended consequence of such a society. For Weber (2001) the cost was to the individual of modernity, what he famously termed the 'Iron Cage'. He warned that "*the fate of our times is characterized by rationalization and intellectualization and, above all, by the disenchantment of the world*", indicating a loss of meaning that accompanies the triumph of calculation. Fisher's work could be read as identifying a modern age intensification of this condition. Whilst Weber may have seen the 'Iron Cage' as being caught up in social functions, Fisher suggests that we have internalised such a cage. Even to the degree that we find our critiques are shaped by the language of managerialism and that our challenges to the system are always part of the system. In the context of psychotherapy, we must question if our focus on locating issues in the individual through diagnostics, in some way, obscures the social and economic determinants of how an individual is impacted by other factors. Under this framing, certain experiences may be understandable responses to external pressures, recognising the economic, social, and political causes of distress (Davies, 2021; Parker, 2007). The implications of which are that therapy becomes a technology for adjusting individuals to conditions that remain unquestioned, reinforcing the very structure that contributes to suffering.

Both Fisher and Weber gesture towards forces that shape conduct without being immediately visible. Whilst Fisher points to an atmospheric quality and background, Weber's term 'spirit' has the essence of an unseen force. Both invite us to consider the ways in which unseen frameworks and cultural influences can lead us to having perceptions and expectations which organise the world around us. This situates psychotherapy as an engagement in the room which is entangled in processes outside of the room. The danger of this sits with the cyclical and engulfing nature of rationality and technology which will be explored through Heidegger.

Technê and Technology'

Understanding that technologies are not autonomous, rather they bear a cultural imprint of society, makes the case that society and technology are in some ways reflective of each other and entwined (Vickery, 1990). But can philosophy in technology offer any insight on how and potentially why these systems interact in such a binding way.

Looking to Heideggerian thinking, there are several key concepts in relation to psychotherapy which might be helpful in developing some understanding of how technology has shaped practice and research over time. In particular, the concepts of 'bringing-forth', 'challenging-forth', 'standing-reserve', and 'enframing' all open ideas which explore the implications for the culture of psychotherapy in relation to manualised practice. This lens will help create a framework from which to explore the relationship a therapist has with method and technique and how this shapes their encounter with their practice. For Heidegger, not understanding this relationship with technology can hinder exploration: "*We shall be questioning concerning technology, and in so doing we would like to prepare a free relation to it*" (Heidegger, 1977. p. 3).

Heidegger is preparing his reader to move from the usual conception of technology as only instrumental towards the anthropological, both a means to an end and a human activity. Whilst he shares the view that this is a correct way to see technology, it is also a superficial way and one which can be concealing of 'aletheia' (a truth). Heidegger wants us to get to the essence of technology and not to the things themselves. As was explored with Weber previously, it is the world view and belief behind the visible that Heidegger is attempting to bring to light. Conventional conceptions about technology as we understand and experience them are correct but are concealing of our true nature as they guide our being in a particular way. Introducing the idea that something is hidden by the everyday superficial and instrumental purpose of technology. We lack awareness of how we interface with technology or at least one aspect of technology, and therefore, we risk a relation to it which can be dangerous. In the case of manualised practice, we can easily become caught up in the efficiency of the technology and with the aim of producing calculable outcomes as a truth. Whilst he is not advocating for a rejection of instrumental technology, he is asking that we begin to recognise that this 'correct' way of viewing technology may stand in the way of a more existential understanding, in turn, concealing as opposed to revealing something about us. This means trying to move beyond the tools and techniques offered to therapists and instead become aware that the way we view the world is affected by how we conceptualise and approach what we are experiencing. If the tools are a mere means to an end for metric outcomes and we do not pay attention, we risk a danger posed not by the superficial technology but, instead, by increasingly denying the ability to feel oneself in an original way. Technology shapes the world around us and, in turn, shapes us into a mode of technological thinking which can propel us further from our sense of

'Being' as a cyclical process, in which we increasingly dominate and shape our environment forcing a particular way of being. As Dreyfus summarises poignantly, "*Heidegger's concern is the human distress caused by the technological understanding of being, rather than the destruction caused by specific technologies*" (1995. p. 26).

To illustrate this, Heidegger brings his reader to a more detailed account in which he explores the term 'Technê' (craftsmanship) in relation to modern technology. The purpose of which is to show in essence that these two forms of technology lend themselves to a very different way of being and engaging with the world. The shift from being a part of a process to controlling the process is for Heidegger our attempt to control and master the world around us. By using Aristotle's four causes, he highlights how we, in the name of production, create with intention and force rather than emerge with. The four causes help us to consider how different components of a process can work in unison to bring something unknown into being rather than forcing the process to steer a predesigned outcome. Below is one way in which we might consider the causes in relation to psychotherapy.

- The Efficient cause – often referred to as the craftsman/the therapist
- The Material cause – that which is to be shaped/the client
- The Formal cause – the form which shapes the material/the technique or modality
- The Final cause – the end point, reason, and purpose/the outcome

Whilst we may think one of these causes more important or relevant, Heidegger brings the notion of indebtedness to them, unifying them and demonstrating that each cause is responsible for bringing-forth from concealment, a form of unfolding. He uses the example of a silversmith to illustrate this process by showing that whilst the silversmith may play a vital role as the 'causa efficient', all the causes belong together in the making (poiēsis). For Heidegger: "*Technê belongs to bringing forth to poiēsis, it is something poetic*" (1977. p. xxiv). However, in the case of modern technology, we are faced with a 'challenging-forth' in which we set upon our environment. We implement a form of ordering to take control of the productive process. Within this "*the revealing that rules in modern technology is a challenging, which puts to nature the unreasonable demand that it supply energy that can be extracted and stored as such*" (Heidegger, 1977. p. 49). In a therapeutic sense, manualised and applied therapies draw out metric outcomes for evidence and further ordering.

The shift from being a part of a process to controlling the process is for Heidegger our attempt to master the world in order that we can extract from it. In this sense, challenging-forth is a way of "driving towards maximum yield and at the least expense" (Heidegger, 1977. p. 49) to unlock and transform what is produced. At this point we begin to store what we have extracted, a term which Heidegger calls 'standing-reserve'. Within this, we cannot see a problem as technology in its instrumental form is working for us and we are able to produce all that we want, but here lies the danger because technological thinking begins to work against us, trapping us, and engulfing us in its cyclical process. We, too, start to become a form of standing-reserve, with expectations to produce and to yield the maximum results. Heidegger uses the term 'Gestell' to represent a form of 'enframing' which takes place in this process. It gathers and engulfs all aspects of the process including the craftsman into a way of being, shaping the world view and order. The greatest danger is that we become bewitched by calculative thinking (Heidegger, 1959). In psychotherapy, examples of this may be therapists working towards targets, feelings of responsibility for outcomes, adapting to models over clients, and even turning away clients who don't meet a metric.

But in relation to the therapist, it would be fair to suggest that this is a complex situation to balance in the therapy room. That in some way we have chosen to undertake a task for and with the other, but that this does not necessarily mean a losing of oneself. Can we show up in a way that redefines us by emerging with clients rather than doing or producing for clients. When exploring improvements and growth of therapists over time, studies have often been orientated around training and education over praxis. One viewpoint even suggested that therapists should not be improving over time but that there should be a direct correlation between training and learning as a measure of growth (Beutler et al., 2004). This sits in direct opposition to writers who advocate that we learn from every individual (Casement, 1985). This articulates a form of openness to being changed by the experiences with the client as a unique encounter each time.

This prompts the question of what is lost and gained through the take-up of method? Exploring how experience changes when moving away from specific directives and methods, towards 'technê' from the Greek understanding of art, craft, or skill (Volti, 2009). Technê sits in the domain of knowledge but one which is different from episteme as it concerns itself with practice and crafting. It is a form of doing and practice which emerges within and from the environment, therefore entwined with the Heideggerian (1977) concept of 'indebtedness' and therefore associated with 'poiēsis' which is a form of emerging with. As such, the term can refer to a source which is unknown to us but yet part of us and unfolds before us. As previously mentioned, there is a danger that technology might come to define our sense of being in the world and in some way conceal from us other truths. Therefore, technê can reveal and offer an 'unconcealment' in a way that modern technology cannot (Heidegger, 1977).

To consider technê as a part of 'Being' articulates one's capacity and potential, rather than distinctly naming or categorising 'Being' as this would be highly problematic. It demonstrates how 'technê' is part of being human and is an unknown and yet to be source of potentiality. It not only speaks to the ability of creation and an openness to possibility but also speaks to the hidden and concealed within us which has not yet emerged. The term is framed from an existential position to demonstrate the alignment between 'Being' and 'Technê' as a coming forth through action and movement. The reason is to demonstrate that 'Being' is entwined with and inseparable to technology in some way. Not necessarily the modern technology we are familiar with but as an action that comes into being and is by that very nature inherently creative. It is expressed in the sense that we can do or make as part of our 'Being' but that this process is inherently ours and comes from oneself. However, it is always arriving in an environment and therefore negotiated and in a state of tension to some degree with the world. Without staying with this tension, we risk following suit and becoming part of a per-established environment which is how therapy is slowly coming to be known. That we are increasingly being asked to produce outcome, rather than be with clients.

To define and instruct what a therapist does and the ways in which one goes about their practice can essentially promote a disconnect from the self to the professional. Simultaneously, showing up and taking one's own unique action without any responsibility to the environment is also equally problematic. It is the tension between these places that is considered as the 'ethical'. We engage with the ethical when we can respond to the environment whilst sustaining the unique and innate capacity of other possibilities available to our 'Being' (Orange, 2014). Our capacity is not to be forgotten if we are to remain open to the world of possibility. This forgetting for Stiegler is already in motion as we consider technology as separate from us. He emphasises the point, "Technicization through calculation drives Western knowledge down a path that leads to a forgetting of its origin, which is also a forgetting of its truth" (Stiegler, 1994. p. 3). He is speaking to the ways in which technical systems and measurements have come to dominate and that we may have forgotten where knowledge comes from. In some ways, this can be considered as a call to remind therapists of *how* they know and *what* they know beyond what the metrics say.

This is a significant point as we start to understand a divergence between a technology which is rooted from within us and is part of our 'Being' and a technology which is externalised and has capacity to detach from us but still call upon us as a resource. This leaves us in a position to ask if we should be educating people on how to carry out and perform being technological themselves or should we be helping people experience and tap into their own sense of self as 'technê'. To build confidence in therapists is to find their voice and style whilst keeping with therapeutic principles and celebrating diversity in practice and research.

To understand psychotherapy simply as a form of technics and tools developed as an external process prompts a forgetting of technics as integral to human existence (Stiegler, 1994). But by viewing technics as our choice, we are encouraged not to anchor ourselves to any one possibility but rather explore the practice of lending ourselves to other possibilities. For Heidegger (1977) this externalisation over time of technology conceals our ability to encounter ourselves in an original way and, as such, places us in the hands of systems and calculative frames which utilise our capacity for its own purpose.

Even theory when held too rigidly can become a form of dominating through analysis if interpretation is given from a place of authority (Sontag, 1964). This serves to defend against unique experience which is always emerging and available to us. Sontag becomes critical of regulated formats for interpretation and a defined language from which to speak of experience "*which illustrates a certain code, certain 'rules' of interpretation*" (Sontag, 1964. p. 3). Whilst her paper is aimed at critiques of art and psychoanalysis, she is exploring our modern tendency to regulate the search for meaning or unconscious meaning beyond the appearances themselves. In essence, we look to theory and sense making to stay grounded or perhaps in the case of therapists at times "*we reach for theory like a fireguard to protect ourselves from the naked heat of what can feel too uncomfortable to bear*" (Meakins, 2012. p. 2). Do we as therapists hold the capacity to take an unconstrained view in psychotherapy or do we potentially hold on too tightly to theory (Brooks, 2008)? This thinking applies to both psychotherapeutic practice and research when asking if space can be created to cultivate thought outside of the methodological margins provided.

References

Bendall, C. McGrath, L. (2020). Contending with minimum data set: Subjectivity, linearity and individualising experience in Improving Access to Psychological Therapies. *Health*. Vol. 24 (1), pp. 94–109.

Beutler, L. E. Malik, M. Alimohamed, S. Harwood, T. M. Talebi, H. Noble, S. Wong, E. (2004). Therapist variables. In: *Bergin and Garfield's handbook of psychotherapy and behaviour change* (5th ed.), pp. 227–306. Wiley. Ed. Lambert, M. J and location is New York, NY

Brooks, O. (2008). "Cultivating the capacity for an unconstrained view": Nietzsche, education and psychotherapy. Philosophical practice. *Journal of the American Philosophical Practitioners Association*. Vol. 3 (2), pp. 285–297.

Casement, P. (1985). *On learning from the patient*. Tavistock Publications. London, England

Dalal, F. (2018). *CBT: The cognitive behavioural tsunami. Managerialism, politics and the corruptions of science*. New York: Routledge.

Davies, J. (2021). *Sedated: How modern capitalism created our mental health crisis*. London: Atlantic Books.

Dobson, K. S. (2010). *Handbook of cognitive behavioural therapies* (3rd ed.). New York: The Guildford Press.

Dreyfus, H. (1995). Heidegger on gaining a free relationship to technology. In: Feenburg, A. Hannay, A. (Eds.), *Technology and the politics of knowing*. Bloomington: Indiana University Press. pp. 25–39

Fisher, M. (2009). *Capitalist realism: Is there no alternative?* Winchester: Zero Books.

Fishman, D. B. Rego, S. A. Muller, K. (2011). Behavioural theories in psychotherapy. In: Norcross, J. C. VandenBos, G. R. Freedheim, D. K. (Eds.), *History of psychotherapy: Continuity and change*, pp. 101–140. American Psychological Association. Washington, DC

Fonagy, P. Roth, A. Higgitt, A. (2005). Psychodynamic psychotherapies: Evidence-based practice and clinical wisdom. *Bulletin of the Menninger Clinic*. Vol. 69 (1), pp. 1–58.

Goldfried, M. R., & Eubanks-Carter, C. (2004). On the need for a new psychotherapy research paradigm: Comment on Westen, Novotny, and Thompson-Brenner (2004). Psychological Bulletin, 130(4), 669–673. https://doi.org/10.1037/0033-2909.130.4.669

Gross, M. L. (1978). *The psychological society*. New York: Random House.

Guilfoyle, M. (2008). CBT'S integration into societal networks of power. *European Journal of Psychotherapy and Counselling*. Vol. 10 (3), pp. 197–206.

Haddock, L. R. (2022). Third-wave cognitive behavioral theories with mindfulness-based interventions. In: Capuzzi, D. Stauffer, M. D. (Eds.), *Counseling and psychotherapy: Theories and interventions* (7th ed.), pp. 217–236. American Counseling Association. Alexandria, Virginia (VA), USA

Heidegger, M. (1977). *The question concerning technology and other essays*, pp. 3–35. Trans: Lovitt. New York: Harper Textbooks.

Heidegger, M. (1959). *Discourse on thinking*. Trans: Anderson, J. M. Freund, H. E. New York: Harper & Row.

Jackson, C. Rizq, R. (2019). *The industrialisation of care: Counselling, psychotherapy and the impact of IAPT*. PCCS Books. Monmouth, Wales, United Kingdom

Kasavina, N. (2017). From theory to technology: The case of existential psychotherapy. *Russian Studies in Philosophy*. Vol. 55 (1), pp. 74–84.

King, L. Moutsou, C. (2010). *Rethinking audit culture. A critical look at evidence-based practice in psychotherapy and beyond*. Ross-on-Wye: PCCS Books.

Layard, R. Clarke, D. M. (2014). *Thrive: The power of evidence-based psychological therapies*. London: Penguin Books.

Loewenthal, D. (2020). Critical existential-analytic, rather than 'evidence based', psychotherapies: Some implications for practices, theories and research. *European Journal of Psychotherapy and Counselling*. Vol. 22 (1–2), pp. 1–8. https://doi.org/10.1080/13642537.2020.1767845

Meakins, E. (2012). *What will you do with my story?* (1st ed.). London: Routledge. https://doi.org/10.4324/9780429484902

Miller, R. (2004). *Facing human suffering: Psychology and psychotherapy as moral engagement*. American Psychological Association. Washington, DC

Miller, P. (2001). Governing by numbers: Why calculative practices matter. *Social Research*. Vol. 68 (2), pp. 379–396.

Narcross, J. Lambert, M. (2018). Psychotherapy relationships that work III. *Journal of Psychotherapy*. Vol. 5, pp. 303–315.

Orange, D. M. (2014). What kind of ethics? Loewald on responsibility and atonement. *Psychoanalytic Psychology*. Vol. 31, pp. 560–569. https://doi.org/10.1037/a0038062

Orange, D. (2011). *The suffering stranger: Hermeneutics for everyday clinical practice*. New York: Routledge.

Parker, I. (2007). *Revolution in psychology: Alienation to emancipation*. London: Pluto Press.

Parker, I. (2002). Universities are not for psychotherapy and counselling training. *European Journal of Psychotherapy, Counselling and Health*. Vol. 5 (4), pp. 331–346.

Pessoa, F. (1991). *The book of disquiet*. Trans: MacAdam, A. New York: Pantheon.

Porter, T. (1996). Making things quantitative. In: Power, M. (Ed.), *Accounting and science: Natural inquiry and commercial reason*, pp. 35–56. New York: Cambridge University Press.

Ruggiero, G, Spada, M. Caselli, G. Sassaroli, S. (2018). A historical and theoretical review of cognitive behavioral therapies: From structural self knowledge to functional processes. *Journal of Rational-Emotive & Cognitive-Behavior Therapy*. Vol. 36, pp. 378–403. https://doi.org/10.1007/s10942-018-0292-8

Shedler, J. (2018). Where is the evidence for 'evidence-based' therapy? *Psychiatric Clinics of North America*. Vol. 41 (2), pp. 319–329.

Shore, S. and Wright, S. (2024). Audit Culture. *How Indicators and Rankings are Reshaping the World*. London, England: Pluto Press Inc.

Smith, J. A. Flowers, P. Larkin, M. (2009). *Interpretative phenomenological analysis: Theory, method and research*. Los Angeles, CA: Sage.

Sontag, S. (1964). *Against interpretation and other essays*. Modern Classics. New York, NY

Stiegler, B. (1994). *Technics and time, 1. The fault of Epimetheus*. Trans: Beardsmorth, R. Collins, G. Stanford, CA: Stanford University Press.

Truijens, F. Zühlke-van Hulzen, L. Vanheule, S. (2019). To manualize, or not to manualize: Is that still the question? A systematic review of empirical evidence for manual superiority in psychological treatment. *Journal of Clinical Psychology*. Vol. 75 (3), pp. 329–343. https://doi.org/10.1002/jclp.22712

Vickery, M. R. (1990). Rhetorical maintenance of technological society: Commercial nuclear power and social orthodoxy. In: Medhurst, M. J. Gonzalez, A. Peterson, T. R. (Eds.), *Communication and the culture of technology*, pp. 137–155. Pullman: Washington State University Press.

Volti, R. (2009). *Society and technological change* (7th ed.). New York: Worth Publishers.

Weber, M. (2001). *The protestant ethic and the spirit of capitalism*. Trans: Parsons, T. Giddens, A. London: Routledge Classics.

4

FROM DISCOVERY TO EVIDENCE

Introduction

> Doubt is not a pleasant condition, but certainty is absurd.
>
> (Voltaire)

As the psychotherapeutic world increasingly equates evidence with numbers, are we under pressure to translate lived experiences into measurable data? This chapter is concerned with the ways in which this widening gap between evidence and experience shows up and shapes research practice and methodology. Rather than treating research as a neutral process that produces knowledge 'out there', separate from the situation and researcher, this chapter takes the position that we are always already part of what we seek to understand. This asks what might be lost when psychotherapy aligns too tightly with calculative forms of thinking and knowledge production?

With the rapid rise of manualised practice, we see a significant shift of practice-based evidence to evidence-based practices. The latter of which is often embedded with frameworks that offer the illusion of certainty and security in a field historically marked by a theoretical plurality and an epistemological uncertainty. In essence, an uncertainty about knowledge itself, understanding that there is a scientism which takes place when there are claims of one reality. This can be problematic when manualised interventions become representative not only of clinical preference but also of institutional necessities derived from administrative and economic demands. Within these systems, psychotherapy is asked to justify itself through metrics from recovery rates to cost-effective analysis, forcing practice and research to reconfigure itself or get out of the line. Slowly we see how psychotherapeutic diversity is eroded into a homogeneous and unquestionable practice, with impact across the board. As recent as this year, the government has been asked to sign a

DOI: 10.4324/9781003651666-4

cross-party letter to support the UK Council for Psychotherapist (UKCP) in their campaign to update NICE guidelines. Their campaign urges for an update to increase access, to widen the range of therapies available, and to consider a broader intake of high-quality evidence which incorporates research beyond randomised controlled trials (RCTs).

This chapter does not seek to dismiss empirical research or deny the importance of accountability within therapeutic practice. Rather it challenges the assumption that scientific rigour equates to methodological fidelity in practice or that psychotherapy can truly be captured through standardised measure alone. In staying fair to the subject matter, it should be noted that evidence-based research is not making such a claim about capturing what matters, its focus is on capturing the totality of earlier research through systematic reviews and RCTs in order that it can inform new studies (https://ebrnetwork.org/about-ebr/). The issue sits not with evidence per se but with a narrowing of what constitutes as 'evidence' and the significant challenges faced in broadening beyond what fits (Rycroft-Malone et al., 2004).

At the core of psychotherapy as previously mentioned lies the therapeutic relationship, which is complex and situated from emerging phenomena that does not conform to diagnostic and measurable standards. Therefore, no manual can truly capture what might emerge in the therapeutic space and so there is a reliance on the therapist to respond to the situation at hand. When adherence to manuals outweighs responsiveness to context and when practitioner knowledge is subordinated to protocol, psychotherapy risks losing contact with its ethical and philosophical foundations.

Whilst research treats psychotherapy as a technical enterprise, the complexity of human experience becomes filtered through methods designed to favour the visible and reportable. Methodology and technique at this stage are no longer merely tools for enquiry but instead become arbiters and gatekeepers of what counts as credible and valid knowledge. Under these conditions, psychotherapy risks losing its discovery-orientated approach if there is a threat to fall outside the boundary of credibility, in turn, forgoing trusting knowledge that emerges from practice itself in favour of empirically validated techniques. The implication of this is that we marginalise the therapist's intuition, and ethical judgement to respond in a helpful way. Even by empirical standards, we know that relational factors account for a greater proportion of therapeutic outcome than any specific intervention.

Preferred Methodology

Within the broad landscape of psychotherapy lies a cluster of approaches which are increasingly preoccupied with demonstrating 'efficacy' through repeatable manualised methods. In this context, RCTs have come to be regarded as the methodological 'gold standard' and their use is steadily becoming the default for both researchers and practitioners (Dalal, 2018; Dobson, 2010). Yet a central concern emerges when we fail to interrogate the paradigms themselves and instead rely on their methodological tools to reinforce and establish claims of 'evidence'. Especially as these methods are not neutral, and they arise from within the very communities seeking to produce knowledge and therefore begin from a pre-established assumption (Kuhn, 2012). For Kuhn, 'normal science' does not simply progress towards objective truth but tends to consolidate and reinforce the existing frameworks. This raises important questions about the nature of evidence-based practice and its implications for practitioners, clients, the therapeutic encounter, and research more broadly (Masfield and Addis, 2001).

Critiques of applying medical model methodologies such as RCTs to psychotherapy are extensive (Dalal, 2018; Elkins, 2009; Miller, 2004; Wampold, 2001). A core challenge is that these approaches frame psychological distress through a disease treatment lens grounded in biological paradigms, rather than a subjective and relational understanding. These epistemological commitments are particularly visible in highly manualised practice that take up diagnostic concepts as the primary focus of treatment. But what happens when interventions which are developed outside the therapeutic relationship and then applied within it? Although some therapists report benefits and find evidence-based treatments helpful when thoughtfully integrated into their work, there remains notable scepticism about practice being shaped by those removed from the realities of the clinical encounter (Chamless, Steward and Stirman, 2012). Moreover, critics argue that an overemphasis on scientific rationality risks "a demoralization of the therapeutic relationship and an atrophy of our sense of human suffering" (Miller, 2004. p. 299), shifting the focus from relational presence towards the delivery of techniques and skills. Essentially, technology in the form of techniques emerges as a dominant factor in the relationship. Increasingly, we see how RCTs are called upon for understanding efficiency from cause and effect perspectives and which offer quantitative interpretations.

There is an argument to suggest that prioritising demonstrable outcomes can in some way constrain discovery and diminish the fluidity of both practice and research, particularly when broader agendas privilege 'evidence' over more pluralistic approaches towards enquiring (Feyerabend, 2010). This is often achieved through quantitative methods which dominate the landscape and which are organised around efficiency and standardisation. However, these structured formats of knowledge production, often in the form of RCTs (Dalal, 2018; Dobson, 2010; Wampold et al., 2017), have been questioned as adequate models for capturing the complexity of psychotherapy (Goldfield, Burkell and Eubanks-Carter, 2010). Despite any ongoing critique and calls for caution, the momentum behind evidence-based practice continues to grow and bind therapeutic services into a system of reportability and homogeneity (Waller, Stringer and Mayer, 2012). With the arrival of artificial intelligence (AI), we can see how these qualities combined with an infrastructure becomes fertile ground for technology to fully take hold and speed up the process if quantifiable evidence continues to count as the only way of knowing.

For several decades there has been sustained resistance towards an overreliance on evidence-based practice and growing calls to recognise the value of practice-based knowledge. This shift reflects an effort towards understanding the therapeutic relationship beyond quantitative metrics and incorporate qualitative enquiry (Geller and Greenberg, 2023; Narcross and Lambert, 2018; Mearns and Cooper, 2020). Greater emphasis is being placed on the relational dimension of therapy and how we can tailor therapy to the unique needs of everyone, acknowledging that there is no single healing component in therapy (Mearns and Cooper, 2020). The notion that there is a specific active ingredient in psychotherapy is disputed, and favour is given to contextual models which offer richer insights than the dominant medical model (Wampold, 2001). Advocating for a form of pluralism and flexibility in the therapeutic encounter, research is increasingly moving its focus towards relational depth and the facilitation of deep authentic encounters in the therapy room (Mearns and Cooper, 2020). This knowledge remains only partially understood, highlighting the importance of continuing research and the development of practice-based evidence in the field.

The concern is that manualised interventions may detract from a nuanced practice-informed understanding of psychotherapy. In this sense, the reliance on treatment manuals highlights how evidence-based treatments work from an empirically narrowed conceptualisation of psychotherapy (Berg and Slaattelid, 2017). We see further criticism levelled up at manualised approaches for their restrictive nature which can impact the capacity and responsiveness of the therapist in real time and situation (Marshall, 2009). While the literature on evidence-based methods continues to expand, comparatively little attention has been given to articulating the lived experiences of therapists working within manualised frameworks. This oversight risks losing a valuable source of knowledge about what constitutes effective psychotherapy in practice.

Here 'effectiveness' is understood beyond the metric impact factor and considered in relation the therapist's capacity to practise in a way that is both informed and responsive to the unfolding context before them. Highlighting the difference both in practice and in research, of what it means to enquire and what it means to seek, "for in inquiry there is no end to be gained and held. Inquiry does not seek answers" (Heaton, 1997. p. 95). We are returned to a more hermeneutic conceptualisation of the therapeutic space in which conversation becomes liberated beyond a pre-designed goal. The implication is a contrast between practices that emerges and adapts within context, and those that are treated as fixed entities to be measured. The challenge to measurement is compounded by a lack of consensus on questions such as what is mental health? And what is the purpose of psychotherapy? (Heaton, 2010). It shows that there is no stable object to study, instead we work from ever shifting definitions which are shaped by those inside and outside of the room. The issue being that when psychotherapy is framed as a problem-solving activity, this can eclipse the openness and possibility available through dialogue.

Despite these complexities, efforts to measure efficacy persist, often accompanied by constraints on clinical practice. Restrictions on what can be considered 'evidence' in clinical research narrow the field of understanding and produces knowledge which can and does translate as a restriction to the therapist. We know these can feel like restrictive practices due to the high rates with which therapists drift away from the manuals. With no feedback loop of what works and doesn't work, difficulties are caused for the science behind the manuals as their deviations become an unknown variable and therefore can make measurement difficult (Waller, Stringer and Mayer, 2012). But what is missed here is a fundamental issue, why do therapists repeatedly deviate from strict manuals, and why is our focus on the compliance of scientific rigour rather than learning from practice? With the increased popularity of RCTs in social sciences beyond medicine, there has been an overreliance and faith in the methodology over enquiry that may be better suited to the field of psychotherapy. Whilst helping bolster confidence in what works, it fails to ask why it works (Deaton and Cartwright, 2024). This does not argue the validity or value of RCTs and empirical research, it merely suggests that they can only ever be part of the picture. Psychotherapy is complex and at times a messy endeavour which is always in motion and therefore will benefit from research that can be fluid and adventurous in its nature. In this sense, we should never reach the full picture as this would mean we have closed something down.

Historically, science is a liberal practice which is a necessity for the growth of knowledge, and therefore, challenging methodological rules and boundaries elicits core discoveries (Feyerabend, 2010. p. 8). This challenges a traditional view of science and its standardised methodological approach as providing reliable and objective frameworks, favouring a more pluralistic approach for enquiring. A similar perspective is shared through postmodernist views which also call for diversity and difference with a particular focus on dialog across difference (Maxwell, 2004). In essence, are we able to dialogue with aspects that feel other to us in an attempt to be changed by discovery and uncertainty?. This also goes beyond ideas of qualitative and quantitative mixed methodology in science and opening psychotherapy to many disciplines which offer insights and create conversations.

As such, could a dialogue between method and non-method invite a creative element to research which does not have a pre-established blueprint. It brings to the forefront the complexity and problematic nature of using method to overcome as opposed to exposing what emerges when there is no directive. Even within phenomenology we see how people like Husserl looked to open a different standpoint by side stepping the 'natural attitude', but he too found himself caught up in method by systematically attempting to put all pre-constituted knowledge out of the way in his phenomenological reduction, a complication noticed by Derrida when he asks if "the phenomenological form of this vigilance Is not already controlled by metaphysics" (1978. p. 5). The importance of this statement is to highlight that when we utilise non-traditional methods to overcome, we can at times find ourselves caught up in a new form of tradition. This brings to light the complications involved in writing and trying to speak of concepts in a way that does not transform them into a detached endeavour. More will be discussed in a later chapter when exploring the method and non-method towards interviews carried out for the research in this book.

Puzzle Solving or Revolutionary Science

Having touched on some of the challenges faced when research is generated for 'evidence', it becomes clear that being drawn into rigid methodologies can create a 'Procrustean bed' for practice. The implications of which are that therapists must then choose between deviating from manuals and replicating a 'cutting off' from their own clients to stay within the frame. We are returned to the question of how we use method to order and dictate research. and if this can at times result in our obtaining knowledge that simply fits a specific paradigm rather than forcing the paradigm to reconstitute itself and embrace the growth in knowledge.

For Kuhn (2012), science holds the possibility of being revolutionary as opposed to a normal science, which "is a solver of puzzles, not a tester of paradigms" (p. 144). The claim of truth is brought into question because normal science does not progress towards ideas of truth as the way we think it does. Instead, method is applied from a foundation which is essentially built by the society attempting to ascertain a particular knowledge and therefore is always starting from a pre-established position. A community is established within a paradigm which conducts its practice without pushing the boundaries and creates adaptation for any anomalies. Within this, steering clear of novelty reinforces the status quo, discovering what it expects to discover (Hacking, 1999. p. xxvi). Meanwhile, revolutionary science has the capability to cause a paradigm shift when anomalies interrupt with unavoidable crisis and turmoil. In evidence-based research, methods might in some way be seen as problem-solving, answering questions such as what works rather than shifting the paradigm into a more revolutionary stance. For example, moving from fixed designs, fixed sample sizes, and end points to models of discovery, which are adaptive, dynamic, evolutionary, and in real time.

It is the formulation of practice into concrete and repeatable forms which becomes problematic rather than allowing elasticity through discovery and a reshaping our understanding. One can even become critical of attempts to utilise hermeneutics as a tool or an ancillary method within the human sciences when this too becomes prescriptive (Applebaum, 2012). This is because things begin to show up as orderable and placed into an inventory or reservoir of options rather than the 'embodied sensibility' of a situation (Wrathall, 2019). It highlights how science can be an alienating practice when dogma and traditional methods are neither challenged nor considered as a paradigm. In essence, the production of rules and processes which give no opportunity for challenge can become a hinderance to the openness of enquiry both in research and in practice. Here, funding and gatekeeping become hurdles towards expanding how we enquire in psychotherapy. Models which prescribe specific practices and then collect data on that practice as previously mentioned reinforce the paradigm as it has labelled knowledge outside of its criteria as redundant. All too often the evidence wars are missing a crucial component, in their bid to show outcome and results towards their own interpretations, they lack an acknowledgement of the complex and irreducible "the ethical meaning of life is ultimately grounded in an ontology premised upon the irreducibly open and inventive rather than on the reductively closed and repetitive" (Meechan, 2019. p. 479).

Again, the use of method is not the issue, it's the lack of space afforded to one's own thinking and exploration. Rigid models whether in research or practice dominate the creative voice with us and bind our thinking to that which came before. We may very well choose to build on what has come before but is there the freedom to wonder and move freely with thought? With this comes a form of hermeneutic courage in which we must risk self-change, vulnerability, tension, and failure in the pursuit of lending ourselves to something other. But that from this, we may gain insight and allow new possibilities to emerge which come direct from the ontological self. This enables a move towards a deregulation and a sense of openness to the personal which can move beyond the inheritance of traditional methods. A reminder that our ways of being and action in the world speak our 'Being' into the world. Through our awareness, there is an opportunity to disrupt and come away from that which is demanded of us, in order that we create space for an unknowable unfolding to occur. Through the fusion of horizons and an openness, we are afforded a form of transcendence that does not come to an end.

Calculative and Meditative Research and Practice

A discussion has emerged regarding the ways in which we follow technical protocol and how we might allow ourselves to expand beyond seeking knowledge to produce outcomes. That we might lend ourselves to encounter knowledge which transforms us within the frameworks in which we work. Exploring these two modes speaks to Heidegger's concept of calculative and meditative thinking. Calculative thinking takes control and is based on a desire to mould the world around us into a particular way. That we produce and quantify the environment to benefit us, associated largely with modern science and technology. Alternatively, there is meditative thinking which aligns itself with meaning and understanding the world as a mystery to be explored and encountered in a non-objectifying way. This form of thinking resists answers of what is and leans into tolerating uncertainty.

It is too simplistic to think of these modes as isolated ways of thinking because they are entangled with the world and do not simply operate as modes that switch off or on. Rather, many factors impact the way we can encounter these modes as we are subject to our environment. However, efficient processes might impact our capacity to take a meditative stance as they seek to smooth over any anomalies, reducing interruptions. These interruptions can be seen as breaks in the process and in a Heideggerian present-at-hand sense; when something breaks, we tend to notice it better. In manualised practices, therapists carrying out interventions may notice that what is on the script of the manual does not always appear in the room. This can at times be seen through the science-practice gap, which is rooted in polarised standpoints regarding a standardised working practice versus an autonomous practice shaped by the encounter (Lees, 2008). Heidegger's (1959) 'calculative' thought might be considered in line with therapists carrying out their techniques; we think we have a grasp on what emerges in the therapy room because we are manoeuvring through it with theory but simultaneously the theory now has a grasp on us, creating a hindrance and dulling our meditative capacities as it forces our actions in some way. For Heidegger it is here that meaning hides itself as "human existence everywhere sees itself challenged-now playfully and now urgently, now breathlessly and now ponderously- to devote itself to the planning and calculating (and navigating) of everything" (Heidegger cited in Wrathall, 2019. p. 19).

The example demonstrates how we might not always know we are caught up in something despite feeling conscious of our choices. That not everything can be seen or known, but that we might always be subject to hidden internal and external forces. Aligning this thought with Fisher's 'atmospheric' concept, we are returned to the idea of pervasive forces which unknowingly shifts our overall direction whilst giving the illusion that we are choosing our way. And so, do we over time find ourselves drifting and keeping up with the current rather than realising that we are moving towards a particular situation? Or do we only become aware when something in the system breaks?

Having explored the ways in which technology as technique has translated into a vast economic and political tool within psychotherapy, the landscape no longer feels a gentle drift but instead is demanding an increasing level of adaption and manoeuvring to stay afloat. Perhaps this is an important time to step back and re-evaluate what matters to us as researchers, practitioners, and people. To remember that our skills, thinking, and perceptions are embodied activities which can shape the ways in which we feel the world (Merleau-Ponty, 2014/1945). As Foucault suggests in his work on technology of self (1994), creating certain practices, particularly in psychotherapy, is akin to our being shaped for the purpose of society rather than embodying practices which encourage us to think differently and as such liberate ourselves. Whilst Foucault raises some key points, he could be critiqued for his essentialising of 'resistance'. That this too risks becoming habitual to some degree, perhaps Foucault's call to keep these practices alive within ourselves is more relatable to staying alert and aware of tensions within us and around us as an ethical engagement. Can we keep openness alive within ourselves and our work taking the view that what we do inhabits our body and bring skills into our bodies (Merleau-Ponty, 2014/1945)? Therefore, the ability to remain open becomes a matter of practice but that if practice becomes dogmatic and calculated, we may subject others to this way of being. Instead, could we resist formulas and scripts, allowing ourselves and clients to "struggle blindly on until, miraculously, thoughts and words become organized by themselves" (Merleau-Ponty, 2014/1945. pp. 369). He demonstrates and allows the emergence of words to organise themselves through a felt sense and ideas to come forth in the encounter. However, in psychotherapeutic practice as we find in research, there are expectations and boundaries which are set for us. And so, we are met with the challenge of allowing ourselves to unfold in some way whilst trying to maintain a tradition and an understanding of our contextual situation. That we must hold both the principles we have set ourselves whilst trying to remain open to what emerges in the therapy room. Trying to tolerate what Ogden (1997) calls 'being adrift' and lending oneself to the encounter at hand. His use and understanding of reveries to locate himself in what might be going on at the unconscious level helps demonstrate this ability to let oneself move with the experience. It is at the relational turn within psychotherapy that the relationship between therapist and client is seen as intersubjective and that the reverie of the therapist is in some way a reflection or telling of what might be emerging in-between. This can also be seen as a form of unconscious communication, but for the purpose of this book, it is being raised as a potential way in which meditative thinking might take place. That we stop taking charge of the conversation or sequencing a narrative and formula but instead allow confusion and uncertainty to be part of the process. Research in the field of reverie whether in methodologies or in the therapy room has received much attention with reference towards its potential for intersubjective experience and therefore provides additional insights from a different source of knowledge (Gee, Loewenthal and Cayne, 2015).

There is a tension which is brought forward regarding how one goes about an encounter which stems from the uniqueness of 'Being' whilst still responding to the other. How can we provide an environment where "words are not used to veil intentions but to disclose realities, and deeds are not used to violate and destroy but to establish relations and create new realities" (Arendt, 2018. p. 200). For Arendt as with Heidegger, there is a danger that within our technological mode of being, the world is increasingly diminishing the space for people to think or be in a way that does not produce but instead create. Psychotherapy therefore becomes a space with immense possibility if one can hold the tension of being with rather than doing to, staying with uncertainty rather than always answering. This offers a space to speak in ways which are not automatic but engaged in the complex, messy, often difficult but authentic and connected.

The human condition of plurality for Arendt is the essential component which can bring about change. She illustrates how, with isolation and lack of speaking together, tyranny can come to rule. Isolated reasoning rather than the political and the plural sets us up to establish arbitrary ethical rules of good and bad which are pre-established and no longer require our engagement. This for Arendt (2018) is a fundamental concern as we no longer take up the realm of the political; instead, we think about the world rather than address how we act within it. Therefore, the ethical demand does not rely on rules but rather the ethical demand arises spontaneously through interactions and therefore through the interconnectedness of human beings and the moral imperative that upholds the well-being of others (Logstrup, 1997). It is, in essence, situational.

References

Applebaum, M. (2012). Phenomenological psychological research and science. *Journal of Phenomenology Psychology*. Vol. 43, pp. 36–72.

Arendt, H. (2018). *The human condition*. Chicago, IL and London: University of Chicago Press.

Berg, H. Slaattelid, R. (2017). Facts and values in psychotherapy: A critique of the empirical reduction of psychotherapy within evidence-based practice. *Journal of Evaluation in Clinical Practice*. Vol. 23, pp. 1075–1080.

Chamless, D. Stewart, R. Stirman, S. (2012). A qualitative investigation of practicing psychologists' attitudes toward research-informed practice: Implications for dissemination strategies. *Professional Psychology: Research and Practice*. Vol. 43 (2), pp. 100–109.

Dalal, F. (2018). *CBT: The cognitive behavioural Tsunami. Managerialism, politics and the corruptions of science*. New York: Routledge.

Deaton, A. Cartwright, N. (2024). Understanding and misunderstanding randomized controlled trials. *Social Science and Medicine*. Vol. 210, pp. 2–21.

Deleuze, G. Guattari, F. (2004). *A thousand plateaus*. New York: Continuum.

Derrida, J. (1978). *Writing and difference*. Trans: Bass, A. Chicago, IL: University of Chicago Press.

Dobson, K. S. (2010). *Handbook of cognitive behavioural therapies* (3rd ed.). New York: The Guildford Press.

Elkins, D. N. (2009). The medical model in psychotherapy: Its limitations and failures. *Journal of Humanistic Psychology*. Vol. 49 (1), pp. 66–84. https://doi.org/10.1177/0022167807307901

Feyerabend, P. (2010). *Against method*. London: New Left Books.

Foucault, M. (1994). *Michel Foucault power: Essential works of Foucault 1954–1984*, volume 3. Ed: Faubion, J. D. Trans: Hurley, R. and Others. London: Penguin Books.

Freud, S. (1995). *The Freud reader edited by Peter Gay*. London: Vintage Originals.

Gee, J. Loewenthal, D. Cayne, J. (2015). Psychotherapy and despair in the prison setting. *International Journal of Prisoner Health*. Vol. 11 (3), pp. 141–56. https://doi.org/10.1108/IJPH-11-2014-0042

Geller, Shari M. Greenberg, Leslie S. (2023). *Therapeutic presence: A mindful approach to effective therapeutic relationships* (2nd ed., pp. 3–12). Washington, DC: American Psychological Association.

Goldfield, M. Burkell, L. Eubanks-Carter, F. (2010). Clinical consensus strategies for interpersonal problems between young adults and their parents. *Journal of Consulting and Clinical Psychology*. Vol. 78 (2), pp. 212–224.

Hacking, I. (1999). *The social construction of what?* Cambridge, MA: Harvard University Press.
Heaton, J. M. (2010). Measurement in psychotherapy. In L. King & C. Moutsou (Eds.), *Rethinking audit cultures: A critical look at evidence-based practice in psychotherapy and beyond* (pp. 37–47). Ross-on-Wye, Herefordshire, England: PCCS Books.
Heaton, J. M. (2014). *Wittgenstein and psychotherapy. From paradox to wonder*. Palgrave Macmillan UK. London, England
Heaton, J. M. (1997). Pyrrhonian scepticism: A therapeutic phenomenology. *Journal of the British Society for Phenomenology*. Vol. 28 (1), pp. 80–96. https://doi.org/10.1080/00071773.1997.11007185
Heidegger, M. (1959). *Discourse on thinking*. Trans: Anderson, J. M. Freund, H. E. New York: Harper & Row. https://ebrnetwork.org/about-ebr/
Kuhn, T. S. (2012). *The structure of scientific revolutions* (50th ed.). University of Chicago Press. Chicago, Illinois (IL), USA
Lees, J. (2008). Research supervision and psychotherapeutic theory: Bridging the research-practice gap. *Psychodynamic Practice*. Vol. 14 (3), pp. 281–293.
Logstrup, K. E. (1997). *The ethical demand*. Notre Dame, IN: University of Notre Dame Press.
Marshall, W. L. (2009). Manualization: A blessing or a curse? *Journal of Sexual Aggression*. Vol. 15 (2), pp. 109–120.
Masfield, A. K. Addis, M. E. (2001). Manual-based treatment Part 2: The advantages of manual-based practice in psychotherapy. *Evidence-Based Mental Health*. Vol. 4, pp. 100–101.
Maxwell, J. A. (2004). Reemergent scientism, postmodernism, and dialogue across differences. *Qualitative Inquiry*. Vol. 10 (1), pp. 35–41.
Mearns, D. Cooper, M. (2020). *Working at relational depth in counselling and psychotherapy* (2nd ed.). London: Sage Publications Ltd.
Meechan, J. (2019). Mechanics that triumph over mechanism: Bergson on the meaning of life. *Human Affairs*. Vol. 29 (4), pp. 479–488.
Merleau-Ponty, M. (2014/1945). *Phenomenology of perception*. Trans: Landes, D. A. London: Routledge.
Miller, R. (2004). *Facing human suffering: Psychology and psychotherapy as moral engagement*. American Psychological Association. Washington, DC, USA
Narcross, J. Lambert, M. (2018). Psychotherapy relationships that work III. *Journal of Psychotherapy*. Vol. 5, pp. 303–315.
Ogden, T. (1997). Reverie and interpretation. *The Psychoanalytic Quarterly*. Vol. 66, pp. 567–595.
Rycroft-Malone, J. Seers, K. Titchen, A. Harvey, G. Kitson, A. McCormack, B. (2004). What counts as evidence in evidence-based practice? *Journal of Advanced Nursing*. Vol. 47 (1), pp. 81–90. https://doi.org/10.1111/j.1365-2648.2004.03068.x
Voltairc (1919). *Voltaire in his letters: Being a selection from his correspondence*. Trans: Tallentyre, H. F. London: Brentano's.
Waller, G. Stringer, H. Mayer, C. (2012). What cognitive behavioural techniques do therapists report using when delivering cognitive behaviour therapy for the eating disorder? *Journal of Consulting and Clinical Psychology*. Vol. 80 (1), pp. 171–175.
Wampold, B. E. (2001). *The great psychotherapy debate: Models, methods, and findings*. Mahwah, NJ: Erlbaum.

Wampold, B. E. Baldwin, S. A. Holtforth, M. G. Imel, Z. E. (2017). What characterizes effective therapists? In: Castonguay, L. G. Hill, C. E. (Eds.), *How and why are some therapists better than others? Understanding therapist effects*, pp. 37–53. American Psychological Association. Washington, DC, USA

Wrathall , M. (2019). The task of thinking in a technological age. In: Wendland, A. J. Merwin, C. Hadjioannou, C. (Eds.), *Heidegger on technology.* New York: Routledge. pp. 13–38

5

FROM CLINICIANS TO TECHNICIANS

Introduction

> We may speak several languages, but one of them always remains the one in which we live.
>
> (Merleau-Ponty)

In previous chapters, we begin to see how psychotherapy has moved into a culture shaped by systems of measurement as it drives towards 'evidence' privileging what can be known and demonstrated. Through conversations about dialogue, science, and '*being with*' rather than '*doing to*', a picture emerges of psychotherapy as a space, not where we suspend knowledge but where we suspend conclusions. Understanding that to stay with only that which can be measured risks an erosion of the complex and the undefinable. This raises the question of what may be obscured or marginalised when calculative modes of thinking dominate practices which are rooted in relational and contextual understanding.

Having traced some of the ways in which psychotherapy has become entangled with framing knowledge as a marketable commodity to be applied and optimised, psychotherapy as a practice is increasingly taking up the idea that there is a correct format or formula to follow rather than an encounter open to endless possibilities. Therapists are therefore encouraged to '*apply*' psychotherapy correctly by following prescribed interventions and established models rather than holding space for what emerges. But under the restrictive nature and conditions of manualised interventions and their implementation, do we become ineffective as therapists (Marshall, 2009. p. 117)?

This chapter takes some of the key implications already mentioned and considers the role and experience of the therapist in more depth. Through existential and phenomenological thought, a perspective is given towards the way in which we navigate our own sense of meaning and autonomy when being

DOI: 10.4324/9781003651666-5

with the other. It helps us to consider therapeutic paradigms which explore the capacity to '*be with*' as the foundational source of ethics and learning in psychotherapy. By redefining '*effectiveness*' as that capacity to hold tension between being informed with theory and holding space for other possibilities to emerge allows a practice rooted in ethics. This invites us to enquire in a way that remains open to possibility and divergence rather than seeking what is known as '*evidence*' and to engage with other forms of knowing or learning which arise from practice itself. Holding space for what is not yet defined and may never be demands a willingness to tolerate this 'being adrift' so that the other might creatively discover meaning and understanding for themselves. In this sense, as therapists we facilitate a space and conditions from which the other can emerge without collapsing into technical and reductive interpretations of experience. This does not dismiss theory and is not an argument for obscurantism but rather resists the totalising demand of 'evidence' and methodology as an absolute authority. It opens up the site of knowing beyond method into the embodied, relational, and experiential, framing psychotherapy as a practice of always learning.

Drawing on a range of existential and phenomenological thinkers in philosophy and literature, this chapter explores the implications of technique as a technology mediating our engagement and experience of the world. It speaks to the increasing treatment of therapists as technicians who carry out a rule-based processes rather than clinicians who can respond authentically and ethically. It is hoped that insights be offered as an invitation to consider our own use of and relationship to technique.

Mediated through Technology

To consider technique as a technic allows us to treat therapeutic practice as a form of technological mediator, which shapes how we see and interact with the world. The development of concepts such as 'mediation theory' (Ihde, 1990) within the philosophy of technology takes the view that different technologies shape our behaviour and knowledge of the world. Ihde and Verbeek's (2016) post-phenomenological theory of 'mediation' offers a framework from which to explore these implications. The framework allows for a pragmatic approach to understanding the first-hand experience of these technologies from the perspective of therapists. This brings to the forefront an understanding of how these technologies in the form of manualised interventions impact the relationship and space between client and therapist.

This philosophy helps relocate technology back to experience rather than gauging outcome through a quantitative rating system based on efficacy. We are reminded that technologies "*belong to the human world in a modality other than that of instrumentality, efficiency or materiality*" (Latour and Venn, 2002, p. 248). The concept of technology beyond an instrumental understanding is considered in relation to the therapist and the impact on their sense of being. Through this lens, high levels of technique mediate the therapist's experience differently from non-technical engagement. Having touched on the lack of evidence showing a marked difference in outcomes for manualised and non-manualised practice, one consideration which is often missed is the impact on the therapist when working with high levels of manualisation.

Through the framework of "mediation", we are introduced to the idea that technologies are a form of media that offer channels between humans and the world around them. When technologies are in use, they shape interactions and relations between the user and the world. Technology being separate as an object or construction and individuals as 'subjects' become problematic because '*technological things*' shape people and affect how people experience their world and organise their existence (Verbeek, 2010). Therefore, technologies carry with them a form of morality, whether intentionally or not, and morality is central to the therapeutic endeavour (Cusworth, 2000).

This framing offers access to a wider scope of questions surrounding psychotherapy (Carroll, 2017) rather than simply looking at the metric of a specific theory or intervention which is often garnered out of context. It allows the social, cultural, ethical, and political implications to become more accessible and incorporated into our understanding the impact on well-being generally. Viewing an intervention as a technology encourages us to ask questions, which we may take for granted with other technologies, such as: Who is the technology for? Who created the technology? Who benefits from the technology? What is the experience of a particular technology? Who is responsible if the technology works or doesn't work? These types of questions are more evident in the philosophy and ethics of technology (Latour and Venn, 2002) but could be helpful in psychotherapy. They open up conversations about power dynamics, ethical responsibility, and cultural shifts, therefore serving as a standard enquiry for transparency within the industry.

The central idea in mediation theory argues that technologies do not simply create the desired interaction between the user and the world but help towards constituting the interaction. Therefore, fixed manualised approaches as a tool shape and constitute the interactions with its user. We are encouraged to ask not only what a technology or technique can do but also how it might influence our existence in the room, regarding where our attention is drawn to and how our interactions have been mediated. To fully understand human-technology relations, we need to firstly see that technologies are in fact not part of the world as an operant but part of our relations with the world. They shape all kinds of relations between humans and the world, and in doing so, they influence practices and the ways in which we perceive the world. Verbeek (2016) takes an example of a sonogram to illustrate what he means with this mediation. He takes the view that the picture of the unborn baby is not just an arbitrary one of a foetus but instead it transforms the relationship between the baby and the parents, and vice versa. The meditation in this case is not between the given entities but instead creates these entities. The sonogram has opened another experience up for the parent as the technology has provided a new channel for experience.

In relation to psychotherapy, diagnosis through calculation for a client begins to constitute a reality for both parties. One might go as far as to say that simply seeing a psychotherapist already brings about a reality when considered as a tool towards a means to an end. This is important for several reasons because it argues technologies shape us rather than being external to us and for our use. They can shape our knowledge of the world, our decision-making, actions, and beliefs as technologies are able to open and close down experiences. Reorganising the boundaries between the given and the made imparts a great deal of responsibility not simply on the design of the technology but also on its use as an ethical and moral stance. Through understanding the importance of technological mediation, we are faced with a responsibility to analyse any impact that our technology or technique may have upon our relationships. Philosophy of technology offers a pragmatic starting point from which to begin understanding the potential effects on experience and interpretation. Four categories are introduced as ways in which technology interacts with humans and how we might experience the world through technology.

Embodied Relations: Technologies that are directed towards the world, but which form a unity with human beings. Ihde gives the example of speaking through a phone rather than at it. This is considered as: (Human-technology) > World.

Hermeneutic Relations: How we register and interpret through technologies as representing something in the world. A metal detector that represents the metal found or a formula or calculation in therapy that represents a condition found. This is considered as: Human > (Technology-World).

Alterity Relations: The way in which we interact with technologies. Our direct interaction with technology whilst the world is in the background. For example, a person will interact with technologies such as robots, artificial intelligence, or cash points in which there is a world behind the mechanics away from direct contact. This is considered as: Human > Technology (World). This book is about the background which sits hidden behind the interaction with manualised manuals.

Background Relations: Context of experience is central here. Technologies which are experienced as background and technologies we might not be aware of in the context or situation, but which serve a purpose. Some potential examples would be oxygen systems on a plane. This is considered as: Human (Technology/World).

Already we can see how mediation theory brings a very pragmatic approach towards understanding our environment and the ways we can experience it. We are encouraged to keep at the forefront the concept of mutual constitution, meaning that technology is not interpreted or felt in any one way as a given (Ihde, 1990). Warning that we can fall into the danger of trying to find and set up a system that constitutes understanding. Whilst we do not want to risk reducing ethics to the rule of technology and as such, should we go beyond technical mediation (Dorrestijn, 2017). It is a good starting point and has begun the conversation at the very least if not already attempted to find a solution.

Introduced is an existential dimension of a hermeneutic nature in which through technologies '*Being*' is present in the world, and the world is present for '*Being*'. Ultimately helping us understand that technologies are not simply tools for outcome but mediators and should not be viewed as an 'object' or technique that is separate. Forcing an examination of how manualised practice organises and shapes the interactions of the therapist becoming mediators of human-world relations. Whilst the work of Verbeek (2016) may be focused on practical technologies, it is the concept that is useful to further explore the implications of manualised technique as a form of technology. By taking a phenomenological stance, there is an attempt to overcome the subject-object dichotomy which has been central to thinking in the past. In this dichotomy, the object is seen as separate to us and merely a utility to achieve any given task. Mediation theory suggests that in using technics, we are in effect shaping the lens by which we experience the world and then having the world returns to us through the parameters of that technology. If we take language as a form of mediating technology and see it simply as a translative tool, then there is a significant narrowing of what become available to us through language. Indeed, when Wittgenstein (1958) speaks of the lion having language, but we would still not understand him, he is challenging this notion that language is simply a set of internal metal codes which can be calculated and understood. He is articulating how language is inseparable to us and the life from which it is used. That different ways of living and experiences attach different meanings to words and therefore never fully graspable. We are therefore encouraged not to see speech, and dialogue simply as a clear representation of what is meant but as an opportunity for hermeneutic courage and discovery rather than certainty and conclusions. This is further explored later in the chapter when considering the complexity of attending to and measuring a multitude of dialogues within us.

In returning to mediation of experience, Heidegger's (1962) concept of '*Dasein*' is helpful in considering how '*being there*' is always directed towards the world, experiencing it and being in it. Simultaneously, the world at the same time is returning to human beings on the basis and foundations of how they relate, incorporating what is meaningful to them. This sits on two dimensions: first, '*hermeneutic*' in the sense of how the world is there for us and from which there is an interpretation of reality. The second is the '*existential*' dimension, which is focused on how we show up in the world. This can be seen as problematic and potentially construed as a dichotomy of its own. Post-phenomenology tackles this by maintaining that human beings and the world co-shape and constitute with each other and within this relation a reality is created in some form. For post-phenomenology, these relations are mediated and so technology can shape the way we encounter the world and how we are in the world. This is an important distinction because rather than measuring the effects of a technique, we are instead invited to examine how the relations and experiences are shaped and mediated by the technology. And so, it is not the effect of a technique that is of interest here but the ways in which how a technique interacts and co-creates with us.

What is proposed is a framework that views psychotherapy as a fluid spectrum from the highly technical and procedural directives to the non-manualised approach which offers no step-by-step guidance. Understanding how technique mediates experience allows us to explore the ways in which different levels of manualised practice impact the effectiveness of psychotherapy from the view of the therapist. For example, a highly technique-driven encounter might require a strong reliance on external instruction and directives of how to be in the therapy room. The implication is that the therapist is carrying out practices which have come about from an external source and so the therapist becomes utilised and directed predominantly from external factors. What then, might it mean to emerge from other possibilities in a way that is not known but spontaneous and in real time? In essence, we don't replicate or produce but rather an environment is facilitated for the client to access any experience available to them and so an 'unfolding' takes place. The term 'Being' is used in its traditional sense in which "*we always conduct our activities in an understanding of Being*" (Heidegger, 1962) and we "*do not know what Being means*" (p. 25). This may at first seem confusing, but it is rather helpful to have a term which is in the world not as a definable 'thing' but as a thing able to avoid definition whilst simultaneously coming forth through motion and time, meaning '*Being*' unfolds.

The Dialogical Self as Unmeasurable

Complex relational theory of the 'dialogical self' centres around the idea that there is an interplay of multiple voices within us, all of which offer diversity in perspectives and encounters with the world (Bakhtin, 2008). This promotes a form of coexistence with all the different perspectives in dialog rather than any self-contained or isolated speech. This highlights how dialog comes alive not only through movement between the voices but also through responses to previous and future discourse. It is here that meaning can be forged in encountering the otherness in the self. Bakhtin favours diversity and creative playfulness in discourse as part of his critique towards "*theoreticism*" becoming dominate. This aligns with Gadamer's concern towards mechanical interpretations or Heidegger's "*Calculative thinking*" in which we encounter the world in a way that is validated through methods as opposed to allowing a new understanding to emerge. Psychotherapy in this sense can be considered as a space which facilitates these dialogues for another whilst recognising one's own dialogue as a potential source of knowledge. Bakhtin (2008) demonstrates the inseparable link between language and self which creates meaning through dialogue. This reminds us of the profound rich tapestry and nature of our inner worlds and our need to connect with ourselves to connect with the other.

The concept of '*heteroglossia*' lends itself to the ways in which a multitude of voices and contexts are present at any one time within us. That language is dynamic and fluid rather than uniformed and measurable in meaning. This does not mean that there are no definitions or formed idea; it means that these are possible interpretations of the world amongst many rather than an objective truth. It is the relationship we have to knowledge and what we do with it rather than knowledge itself. Bakhtin's use of '*centripetal force*' can be seen as the social and ideological forces which attempt to unify and centralise meaning akin to that of the 'self' being technological. These forces attempt to standardise and legitimise language in opposition to 'centrifugal forces' which disperse and diversify meaning. In essence, what Bakhtin (2008) is demonstrating is the back-and-forth process that we might encounter when reconstituting meaning through a diversification of our thinking and speaking. This is carried out by opening the potentiality and tension held in language which reflects how we might often be communicating social ideologies in our discourse (Packer, 2018). Through these tensions there is no one truth but an ongoing disclosure in a somewhat truthful manner, and we might start to make sense of things for ourselves (Grubel, 2015). These ideas are very close to some of the Heideggerian (1962) concepts already spoken about, we are reminded of '*Aletheia*' which is a form of disclosure or unfolding.

Martin Buber's (2013) 'I-Thou' and 'I-It' can be a helpful way to consider how we might engage with the other in a way which obscures or hinders possibilities from emerging. The 'I-Thou' speaks of an embracing engagement with otherness in such a way that we meet the other in all its uniqueness, not the perceived or known, but in what emerges in the moment. Contrary to this, the 'I-It' expresses a relationship in which the other is categorised and imposed upon by one's own framework. Heidegger's (1977) concept of 'enframing' echoes the idea that our mode of thought can shape the way we impose our frameworks onto nature and the world around us. It prompts consideration towards the question, can the meaningful presence of 'things' become obscured by technique in the context of manualised practice?

What is attempted is to resist the authority given to any one utterance or singular voice whether it be external or internal but instead recognise the dynamic interplay between them. By holding the tension between traditions and expectations and making space for otherness, every voice has the potential to be its own genre (Derrida, 1978). For psychotherapy, it highlights the potential difficulties faced by therapists when developing their internal voice as its own authority over external systems which dominate (Pollard, 2008). Can we resist the theory and technique to show up and respond to what is emerging in a relational way rather than an automatic manner.

So how might we explore this openness to alterity within us? And what are the complexities that come with unfolding, disclosing, and encountering otherness and uncertainty? If starting with a Levinasian ethics, we might begin with dismantling ongoing attempts to conceptualise and categorise the '*Other*' who expresses themselves in a way that we cannot grasp (Lévinas, 1967). To resist the persistence of placing discoveries within a totalising system which makes everything known, and which closes down or distances our encounter with the '*Other*'. Therefore, the '*Other*' appears fundamentally separate from me and yet with me, no longer a concept or category but rather as a world of immense and profound possibilities. Knowing is perfectly reasonable and very much needed in psychotherapy, but it is the totalising nature of theory that becomes problematic. For Lévinas, the 'Other' is about the unknowable, the infinite which is interminable:

> Other at each moment destroys and overflows the plastic image it leaves me, the idea existing to my own measure and to the measure of its ideatum—the adequate idea.
>
> *(Lévinas, 1967. p. 51)*

So, what is meant by alterity when thinking about Lévinas? It lets us know that the '*Other*' cannot be known in a qualitative or quantitative way. By this it means that the '*Other*' cannot be brought into recognition or sameness by becoming aware of qualitative or quantitative differences between the self and other. The relationship between same and '*Other*' cannot be bridged through a reducible disclosure as they do not sit in opposition to each other. Philosophy for Lévinas has reduced the '*Other*' to the same through a variety of means and methods without accounting for the 'irascibility of alterity'. This has resulted in a closing down of the ethics to respond to the 'Other' as philosophy has failed to start with ethics as the first philosophy. The idea of the infinite within us is in some way a proof that the infinite exceeds us.

This does not mean that taking up any kind of understanding is wrong, rather it simply asks that we remain open in our encountering of the '*Other*' without collapsing it back into the same and without trying to reduce to sameness (Orange, 2009). We should recognise the 'Other' as a universe of mystery to us or better still simply not recognise the '*Other*' but respond as it calls to us (Lévinas, 1967). However, what of the 'Other' within us? Might we take an ethical consideration towards our own otherness, the parts of ourselves we don't grasp (Ricoeur, 1992). The '*Other*' challenges our automatic ways of doing things and emerges through an openness to the unknowable. There is a potential connection between a form of '*self-responsibility*' and what Lévinas articulates as '*for-the-other-responsibility*' (Orange, 2014). From this standpoint we might consider that whilst there is responsibility to the '*Other*' in the therapy room, practitioners also hold a responsibility to the ungraspable within themselves, a commitment to attend to one's unfolding and freedom. If we are to consider how this '*freedom*' might be thought of as the ability to surpass a givenness in an open future full of possibilities (De Beauvoir, 1947/1976), might the practitioner's own ability of '*freedom*' condition the therapeutic situation for others?

For Foucault (1994) it is a breach of self-evidence which he deems as "*making visible a Singularity at places where there is a temptation to invoke a historical constant, an immediate anthropological trait, or an obviousness that imposes itself uniformly on all*" (p. 227). Whilst encouraging an openness to these encounters, there is a sense that how this happens is both personal and unique. His work on 'technology of self' (1994) highlights how there is a way of cutting off from the '*Otherness*' in us through regulated practices which lend themselves to a uniformed way of being. However, we must take care of what awaits us in this unknowable and ungraspable place. For here lies the potential 'abject' and a breaking through of one's constructed identity which is set upon the boundaries we create between the self and the other. For Kristeva (1982), anything which transgresses or falls out of these boundaries must face a radical exclusion as it brings with it a threat to our identity, experienced as the abject and provoking repulsion.

Authenticity and 'Bad Faith'

In the landscape of psychotherapy, models which are increasingly filled with directives and efficiency systems, how might we come to understand our choices and does the way we choose reveal something about us? For Kierkegaard (1946), an "*existing individual is constantly in process of becoming*" (p. 115) not in the sense of becoming something objectively discovered or grasped necessarily, but an ongoing task shaped through lived choices and a task which remains unfinished. In this sense, we are always encountering ourselves or at least have the opportunity if we engage with an awareness of the choices we make. In an existential thought, authenticity is often positioned as a taking up ownership of one's choice and existence rather than passively living in the '*das man*', the they-self, a state in which we live according to the traditions and expectations of a given culture or, in the case of psychotherapy, the professional norms. There is a call to awareness for the ways we engage and how lending ourselves to the automatic may be seen as a disengagement from our own potentiality.

It is this lack of awareness that can result in us entering what Sartre (1956) calls "Bad Faith" a form of self-deception in which we tell ourselves we are determined and governed in our choices because we are a particular thing. This is not a difficult place to fall into when starting as a therapist given how much uncertainty there is in the room and how manuals and theory offer a system on how to be. Through Weber and Heidegger, we have begun to see how a way of looking at the world can become part of a cyclical nature in which our ideas shape our environment but without attention our environment starts to shape us. This mechanical-like process engulfs the individual and culture into a particular way of being. However, there is always the ability for the autonomous to change these processes. But this does not appear so easy and often there may be a cost associated with psychotherapy as training, employment, accreditation, and legitimisation all place a demand on access. This is not to say that institutions should not have rigorous and high standards of practice. Quite the opposite, it is to say that promoting critical thought and self-awareness is equal if not more ethical than teaching directives and absolutes. The evidence-based paradigm positions itself as an authority through metrics; phenomenological thought transcends the idea of knowledge being situated in a particular paradigm and allows access to all lived experience. This can indeed feel overwhelming and so we find ourselves grasping at organising structures such as rationality which only becomes problematic if it is the only way we come to know the world.

A poignant story which comes to mind is that of the underground man by Fyodor Dostoyevsky (2020), a character who cannot bear himself. We are entered into a dystopia from an enlightened society, in which our protagonist finds himself in a constant state of flux. He is crippled by his consciousness, and his use of rationality binds him in a way that leaves him in a state of inertia. He finds himself unable to choose as he cannot be certain of his choice before he has made it. In failing to find reasonable purpose to begin, he is caught out by his own thinking and the demands placed on his reasoning. Furthermore, he cannot be sure that the primary purpose he chooses is his own rather than a secondary one. He gives a damning account of how we have come to rationalise values as though they were a fixed and knowable thing; "*You, gentlemen, have so far as I know, drawn up your entire list of positive human values by tackling the averages of statistical figures and relying on scientific and economic formulae*" (Dostoyevsky, 2020. p. 21).

This is a commentary on the division between the external rational world he is a part of and the internal landscape in which he hides. He centralises the conflict between how one knows oneself and desires in a rational way and how one might never fully grasp their experiences or actions. Dostoyevsky speaks of the man of action and the man of intelligence to illustrate this. What is inescapable in his work is the fear and anxiety that runs through the protagonist as he contemplates becoming a man of action, one who acts without thinking, almost in a whimsical way. A theme which is also found within the work of Kierkegaard as he says, "*If anyone on the verge of action should judge himself according to the outcome, he would never begin*" (1985. p. 74). We are returned to the idea of knowing in different ways, an acquiring of knowledge, and a knowledge yet to be discovered within ourselves through action. For Kierkegaard, this distinction sits in two realms, knowledge as a possibility and the ethical; "*Abstract thought requires him to become disinterested in order to acquire knowledge; the ethical demand is that he become infinitely interested in existing*" (Kierkegaard, 1941. p. 117).

What is significant here is the way Kierkegaard expresses how the existing individual is always in a state of becoming, and as such, any abstract notion of identity is merely what he calls "*a chimera of abstraction*" (Kierkegaard, 1941. p. 115), a somewhat quasi-identity. Implications are made towards the individual falling into some form of game, the game of humanity:

> And when one finds that every cellar-dweller can play the game of being humanity, one learns at last, that being purely and simply a human being is a more significant thing than playing the society game in this fashion.
>
> *(Kierkegaard, 1941. p. 115)*

The statement 'playing the society game' once again alludes to an external playing field in which there is a conflict with the self and our environment. The theme of authenticity and knowing oneself in a way that is not conceptualised has played a central role in psychotherapy and existential literature. For Sartre (1956), yielding to external pressures is a disowning of one's authentic self and the freedom bestowed upon them. How we might bind ourselves to external moral and ethical systems which relinquish us from the freedom of choice one has in the world.

It speaks to the idea that there is always a multiplicity of voices with us from the world that it can risk drowning out a sense of oneself without even knowing. A situation Kierkegaard warns against when he says, "*The greatest danger, that of losing one's own self, may pass off as quietly as if it were nothing; every other loss, that of an arm, a leg, five dollars, a wife, etc., is sure to be noticed*" (1946. p. 49).

Authenticity as an existential notion asks that we own and take responsibility for becoming aware of our words, choices, and histories. As such, a warning towards what Stiegler (1994) calls a 'blind trust' in the functionality of the system or in the name of evidence and science, not because it can't be trusted, quite the opposite as its incredibly useful, but because 'blind trust' encourages a disengagement of sorts to maintain a system. To remain ethical then, we are encouraged to engage with theories and evidence as possibilities rather than concrete applications. For Arendt (2018), it is the contemplative life, a tradition she firmly roots with Plato which has caused us to predominantly think about the world rather than address how we act within it. Arguing that there are two core ways in which people are in the world: the contemplative and the active life (Arendt, 2018). Arendt breaks down active life (vita activa) into three main areas: labour, work, and action. It is 'work' and 'action' which predominantly draw in implications for practice. Taking us from a static conceptualisation of the world to one which is socially constructed and in motion. She moves from an essentialising system which could be seen as 'labour' to one in which is shaped and conditioned.

Action for Arendt is involved with the new, and from it comes a form of uniqueness as a possible outcome. It is aligned and caught up with speech and with the possibility of revealing a uniqueness (Arendt, 2018). This action is important for Arendt because it is in this action that we are revealing something about ourselves and creating something new, also seen as a form of '*becoming*'. That we live in the world with others and whilst we may share many similarities and ways of being, we are always capable and distinct enough to create our own sense of the world. It is here that we consider the role of the therapist both as a person who is also always '*becoming*' in the world and as a therapist playing a role in the world.

References

Arendt, H. (2018). *The human condition*. Chicago, IL and London: University of Chicago Press.

Bakhtin, M. (2008). *The dialogic imagination. Four essays*. Trans: Emmerson, C. Holquist, M. University of Texas Press. Austin, Texas (TX), USA

Buber, M. (2013). *I and Thou*. Trans: Smith, R. G. London: Bloomsbury Academic.

Carroll, L. S. L. (2017). A comprehensive definition of technology from an ethological perspective. *Social Sciences*. Vol. 6 (4), pp. 1–20. https://doi.org/10.3390/socsci6040126

Cusworth, S. (2000). Moral knowledge and the problems of psychotherapy. *Journal of Theoretical and Philosophical Psychology*. Vol. 20 (1), pp. 25–35.

De Beauvoir, S. (1947/1976). *The ethics of ambiguity*. Trans: Frechtman, B. New York: Citadel Press.

Derrida, J. (1978). *Writing and difference*. Trans: Bass, A. Chicago, IL: University of Chicago Press.

Dorrestijn, S (2017). The care of our hybrid selves: Ethics in times of technical mediation. *Found Science*. Vol. 22, pp. 311–321. https://doi.org/10.1007/s10699-015-9440-0

Dostoyevsky, F. (2020). *Notes from underground*. Trans: Garnett, C. London: Global Classics.

Foucault, M. (1994). *Michel Foucault power: Essential works of Foucault 1954–1984*, volume 3. Edited by Faubion, J. D. Trans: Hurley, R. and Others. London: Penguin Books.

Grübel, R. (2015). Bakhtin's theory of speech genres and the addressivity in cultural pragmatics of genres in literature: "Genus" vs. "Genre". Umjetnost riječi: Časopis za znanost o književnosti, izvedbenoj umjetnosti i filmu (The Art of Words: Journal of Literary, Theatre and Film Studies), 59(3–4), 215–238. Zegreb, Croatia

Heidegger, M. (1977). *The question concerning technology and other essays*, pp. 3–35. Trans: Lovitt. New York: Harper Textbooks.

Heidegger, M. (1962). *Being and time*. Trans: Maquarrie, J. London: SCM Press.

Ihde, D. (1990). *Technology and the lifeworld. The Indiana series in the philosophy of technology*. Bloomington: Indiana University Press.

Kierkegaard, S. (1946). Concluding unscientific postscript. In: *A Kierkegaard anthology.* Princeton University Press. Bretall, R. W, Princeton, New Jersey (NJ), USA, pp. 190–258

Kierkegaard, S. (1941). Concluding unscientific postscript. In: Friedman, M. S. (1991). (Ed.), *The worlds of existentialism: Critical reader* (2nd ed. with new preface). Atlantic Highlands, NJ: Humanities Press International, pp. 114–117

Kierkegaard, S. (1985). Fear and Trembling (A. Hannay, Trans.). London, England. Penguin Books (Original work published 1843).

Kristeva, J. (1982). *Powers of horror. An essay on abjection*. New York: Columbia University Press.

Latour, B. Venn, C. (2002). Morality and technology. *Theory, Culture and Society*. Vol. 19 (5–6), pp. 247–260. https://doi.org/10.1177/026327602761899246

Lévinas, E. (1967). *Totality and infinity: An essay on exteriority*. Trans: Lingis, A. Pittsburgh, PA: Duquesne University Press. (Original work published 1961).

Marshall, W. L. (2009). Manualization: A blessing or a curse? *Journal of Sexual Aggression*. Vol. 15 (2), pp. 109–120.

Merleau-Ponty, M. (2017). *Phenomenology of perception*. Trans: Smith, C. London: Forgotten Books.

Ogden, T. (1997). Reverie and interpretation. *The Psychoanalytic Quarterly*. Vol. 66, pp. 567–595.

Orange, D. M. (2014). What kind of ethics? Loewald on responsibility and atonement. *Psychoanalytic Psychology*. Vol. 31, pp. 560–569. https://doi.org/10.1037/a0038062

Orange, D. (2009). *Thinking for clinicians*. New York: Routledge.

Packer, M. J. (2018). *The science of qualitative research* (2nd ed.). Cambridge: Cambridge University Press.

Pollard, R. (2008). *Dialogue and desire. Mikhail Bakhtin and the linguistic turn in psychotherapy*. London: Karnac Books.

Ricoeur, P. (1992). Oneself as another. Trans: Blamey, K. Chicago, IL: University of Chicago Press.

Sartre, J. P. (1956). *Being and nothingness a phenomenological essay on ontology.* Citadel Press: Kensington Publishing. New York, NY

Stiegler, B. (1994). *Technics and time, 1. The fault of Epimetheus.* Trans: Beardsmorth, R. and Collins, G. Stanford, CA: Stanford University Press.

Verbeek, P. P. (2016). Toward a Theory of Technological Mediation: A Program for Postphenomenological Research. In J. K. B. O. Friis & R. P. Crease (Eds.), *Techno-science and Postphenomenology: The Manhattan Papers* (pp. 189–204). Lexington Books. Lanham, Maryland (MD), USA

Verbeek, P. P. (2010). *What things do: Philosophical reflections on technology, agency, and design.* Penn State Press. University Park, Pennsylvania (PA), USA

Wittgenstein, L. (1958). *Philosophical investigations* (3rd ed.). Trans: Anscombe, G. E. M. New York: Macmillan.

6

WHAT THE THERAPISTS SAY

Introduction

> I think the meaning of psychotherapy is love.
>
> (Interviewee)

Having considered ideas of how therapy goes about inquiring, discussions have centred around the use of methods and the implications of highly systematised environments for research and practice. This brings to the forefront questions about a therapist's engagement with method and technique in attending to the other. And how complex layers such as hermeneutics and mediation become entangled in perspectives and experiences, in and about psychotherapy. With large quantities of research geared towards quantitative evidence identifying effective therapies, psychotherapy is losing deeper understanding that can be more socially and contextually rooted (Saxon, Firth and Barkham, 2017; Wampold et al., 2017).

Having brought an existential and phenomenological lens to some of the cultural shifts we have seen in psychotherapy, this chapter explores first-hand how therapists navigate their relationship to technique and manualised approaches. Through phenomenological research carried out with 12 therapists, in-depth interviews offer an experiential component which feels honest, direct, and representative of the conditions and complexities faced in the field of psychotherapeutic work. The interviews allow a more nuanced and less audited version of how therapists relate to their practice. This aligns with a conversational style and allows a more informal and personal approach whilst still maintaining its purpose and structure under qualitative standards (Bogdan and Biklen, 2007; Blaxter, Hughes and Tight, 2001; Warren, Townsend and Quigley, 2022). The move towards a conversation and away from controlled standards of quantitative inquiry gives a sensitivity and intimacy which can lend itself to encountering knowledge from a questioning and listening approach. As this is a topic which is not often explored in-depth, interviews

DOI: 10.4324/9781003651666-6

offer greater space and time for participants to consider their thoughts. However, the interviews are still structured insofar as they are planned, timed, and bring about focus on a specific topic introduced with purpose.

As part of remaining with the ethos of the book, the interviews are not focussed on producing certified outcomes, and they are positioned as discovery-oriented. Whilst this may sacrifice a form of applicability and quantitative significance, they allow space for more complex phenomena to emerge. Understanding that losing the ability to make universal statements through quantitative 'evidence' does not detract from the level of validity that comes with a qualitative inquiry. The advantage of letting go of the 'evidence' means that space is made for dialogue and curiosity rather than finding certainty. In addition, it allows a refocus from producing outcomes to exploring experience as a discovery-orientated endeavour and simultaneously understanding the dilemma of being able to honour what is said whilst still allowing the research to follow its course (Hastings, 2010). The limitations of this book cannot give justice to the full interviews, and the interviews themselves cannot give justice to the scope of thought and meaning which the therapists experience. Instead, we are given a descriptive snapshot of a moment in experience from which we can encounter a sense of how therapists navigate their relationship to the landscape of manualised practice. Stories of disbelief, frustration, heartbreak, burnout, and the power of magic in the relational all come together to give new insights into what is helpful and what hinders therapeutic practice.

With limitations to space came another dilemma, how to present the conversations. An active decision was made to replace direct verbatim with overviews and descriptions of the conversations at hand. This choice means more can be presented within the scope of the book and so key elements of the interviews are given voice over direct quotes. Descriptions of themes which emerged have priority over interpretation and come directly from the interviewees themselves.

Designing the Research

The initial design and strategy of the research at its core was motivated to explore the notion of 'effectiveness' from a qualitative and experience-led framework. Whilst a small sample size in the quantitative world of research, the research offered a rich and in-depth insight into the world of psychotherapy, laying the ground for wider and ongoing inquiry. This is because a discovery-oriented approach does not necessarily seek to answer but instead open discussion, understanding, and insights that metrics cannot obtain. Intentionality remains open to current and new knowledge rather than articulate evidence, therefore better reflecting the philosophy and ethos of this book.

With the aim to invite lived experiences, qualitative studies are often considered suitable choices (Packer, 1989; People, 2021; Smith, Flowers and Larkin, 2009). The interviews delve into the practices of therapists and give first-hand accounts and descriptions of how they see and experience the therapeutic space during varying levels of manualised encounters. There is a commitment to the participant's understanding of the phenomena as qualitative methodologies present findings in a literary style closely entwined and rich in participant commentaries (Streubert-Speziale and Carpenter, 2007). Giving voice to the people at the centre of the phenomenon helps us to better understand what draws them to and away from technique in psychotherapy. It enquires about their experiences and sense of self in relationship to the core topic.

A phenomenological approach was chosen due to its central focus on experience. There are several options available in qualitative phenomenological research which offer a range of advantages and disadvantages. In this case, the interviews were carried out using Giorgi's highly technical and methodical approach 'Descriptive Phenomenological Analysis' (DPA). There were several reasons for this selection, in particular, DPA offers rigour whilst not sacrificing or reducing the participants to any one theory or framework. The intention of using Giorgi's (1997, 2009) method of analysis is to provide a phenomenological perspective whilst simultaneously demonstrating a highly manualised and technical approach to the interviews. Whilst there are creative elements within the approach such as the practice of 'imaginative variation' alongside a sensitivity to the discipline of psychology when re-describing the data, it is the step-by-step formulaic approach which offers a manualised and empirical aspect to the method. This choice was purposeful as it offered a method which runs parallel with the discussion found in this book. DPA offers all the benefits of phenomenological enquiry whilst providing a highly technical and in many ways manualised approach. Within the research carried out, DPA was used as the counter point to a non-methodological engagement with the interviews. This offered the research its own lived understanding of how method interacted with practice. What does it mean to say non-method and does such a thing exist? As researchers, we are often given numerous methods to follow but here there felt an opportunity to create one's own style of thinking. The interviews after a methodical analysis were then encountered from my own framework of principles which felt relevant. From this emerged poetry, music, essays, and free associations which embedded me as a researcher into deeper personal reflections and understanding of my own relationship to technique and method in practice. And so, the non-methodological approach towards the research came from a place without blueprint or instruction, creating uncertainty but more importantly making space to be creative. This lending oneself to the research brought about a deeper understanding of what it means to venture into unknown territory. Bringing with it a first-hand experience of how method in the research mediated my own relationship to the interviews giving both an analytical and ontological position, which was captured through a journal. These writings have been left out of the book to give more space for the voices of other therapists.

Of course, there were many other phenomenological avenues which could have been chosen for the research such as 'Interpretive Phenomenological analysis' (IPA) (Smith, Flowers and Larkin, 2009) and 'Heuristics' (Moustakas, 1994, 1990). Both of which are hermeneutical methods in the sense that they prioritise praxis over theory and are considered as a-theoretical (Hastings, 2010). Seen as a hermeneutic endeavour in which creativity and flexibility are prioritised over method and technique, these were feasible options. Another possibility included discourse analysis which centres itself around communication and offers a systematic framework from which to explore the ways in which language reflects identities, power dynamics, and social constructs (Eagleton, 2008). Through unravelling layers of communication, discourse analysis delves into hidden meaning and structures which are embedded in communication (Ayton, Tsindos and Berkovic, 2023; Packer and Addison, 1989). This holds the premise that language is not a neutral tool to convey information but rather a social practice which is intertwined with power and ideology. Its examination of language both written and spoken is often explored in the larger context and therefore includes the social, historical, and situational factors that shape the interpretation of discourse. Underpinning its philosophy is the idea that reality is socially constructed and that the ways in which we dialogue can shape our perception (Smith, 2009).

So why choose DPA when there are hermeneutic implications involved in research which can be resolved by methodologies such as IPA? Because as a researcher, it felt important to be exposed and develop one's own understanding of how highly technical methods shaped engagement to the research. Through other methods, a blueprint would be given to understand this engagement, legitimising through method rather than remaining open to other possibilities in research and potentially psychologising phenomenology itself (Loewenthal, 2020). This makes a return to Heidegger's (1977) warning that we cannot use technology to escape technology, rather we must understand our relationship to it. We cannot escape technology and method, predominantly because it is part of being human (Stiegler, 1994).

Therefore, understanding engagement with method and techniques helps to remain open, and staying with any tensions which arise could be seen as an ethical approach (De Beauvoir, 1947/1976) and one which encourages an ongoing critical stance. This stance is not to remove or destroy anything that has been built method wise, but rather that we continue running the borders of theory and practice, in the hope that we can attempt to always have some awareness of our 'embeddedness' to the situation which presents. This requires that we acknowledge how we are in some ways always entangled in the method, theory, and practice rather than separate from it (Willig, 2008). By understanding that psychotherapeutic research already exists in relation to technology and method (Vickery, 1990) we are in some way freed up to explore the technological within us (Stiegler, 1994).

The Method

Giorgi's (1997) 'Descriptive Phenomenological Method' (DPA) was selected for several reasons due to its clarity and holistic approach to phenomenology. His 1997 article appeared as his most formulaic and process-driven description of his method. The article encapsulates the method and offers researchers the most robust structure available, being rooted in philosophy whilst having a respect for the rigour required in modern-day science. By keeping the principles of philosophical phenomenology and adapting it to meet the rigour of modern-day science, Giorgi can give this method a more central role within the scientific community.

Giorgi (1997) offers an initial overview of his five-step approach to conducting the research:

> (1) Collection of verbal data, (2) reading of the data, (3) breaking of the data into some kind of part, (4) organisation and expression of the data from a disciplinary perspective, (5) synthesis or summary of the data for purposes of communication to the scholarly community.
>
> *(p. 7)*

Therefore, the findings are presented following Giorgi's (1997, 2009) empirical method of analysis which places an emphasis on eliciting findings from a phenomenological reductive stance (epoché) that does not interpret the data but rather describes the experience as it appears to the participant. The core aim of the method is to elucidate what the essential structures or themes are within the data and therefore understanding the essential structures to the phenomenon. What Giorgi means by essential structure and themes is to understand which core characteristics are essential for the phenomenon not to 'collapse' (Giorgi, 1997, 2009).

This book does not hold the space for a detailed and more complex understanding of Giorgi's method as it wants to give space to the themes which have emerged from the therapist interviews. All 12 therapists are qualified practitioners, and several are supervisors in current practice, with experiences across a range of institutions. These include NHS Talking Therapies, Child and Adolescent Mental Health Services (CAMHS), mental health charities, schools, digital platforms, insurance, universities, and their own private work.

Reduction Overview for Each Conversation

The following segment explores a synthesised version of each individual therapist and their interview using DPA. The reduced general synthesis will be presented, and then a general synthesis for all participants will be shown. Again, this allows the reader to gain an overall insight into each individual participant and general framing of the data collected. Within the research an eidetic reduction is carried out to capture the essential structures of consciousness towards the phenomenon, but, for the purpose of this book, an overview is given rather than the reduced version to capture the essence better.

The chapter then explores key themes which emerged from all the interviews and from the synthesis. The breakdown of themes incorporates eight core structures which have been identified as essential to all the data.

Therapist 1 – 'Environments for Practice'

Environmental conditions are central to good practice and a sense of freedom in practice. There is great merit in therapeutic tools and practices that are considered manualised but delivered under certain conditions can become difficult to engage with and testing of any therapist. Frameworks, services, and cultural environments that are restrictive and geared towards achieving their own agenda can compromise connectivity with self and the client. They can prevent the therapist from deep therapeutic engagement and care for their clients as there is little space and time for building trust and honesty. With no room for adaptation or personalisation of interventions and manualised models, practice feels hindered and pushed towards external knowledge which cannot always be fulfilled as opposed to in the moment relational knowledge which feels just as important. There is an active avoidance to work within any environment or service that does not allow space or freedom to bring a fuller practice and experience to sessions. Environments that place such pressures without appropriate support can feel chaotic and unorganised and can have a potential trickle-down effect on the clients.

Therapist 2 – 'Learning through the Here and Now'

There is an importance to living in the moment rather than existing as it offers an opportunity to be in touch with varying dimensions of oneself. This is helpful not only for the client but for the therapist as they too are on a journey of growth and learning. For the therapist there is an essential component of reaching out and exploring experiences from a place of being in the experience rather than thinking about it. It is through engagement with these different aspects of the self that learning and discovery happen. Stepping into training and for the therapist on a personal level has felt difficult and also rewarding when she could step into herself and challenge her own negative beliefs of herself. Through this she has discovered how she is drawn to people's variations and twist on ideas but how narrow training can be and that with no diversity can feel strained and exhausting. This she applies to her own practice and feels encouraged to see practice more as an art form from which creative and unique experiences can emerge. Having struggled with racism within the profession, the therapist feels there are different types of knowledge, which is learnt and which is experienced. People as individuals should shape practice rather than practice shaping the individual, the position of the therapist is to be on the journey with the client as they build trust in responding in the moment. This she sees as a similar trait for training therapists. They should be able to bring their own individuality to shape and mould as a collective rather than one interpretation of theory.

Therapist 3 – 'Freedom and Power to be Oneself'

Psychotherapy is presented as having a multitude of aims which can change at any given moment. Freedom and liberation to be oneself is central as psychotherapy is a movement towards becoming oneself. Manualised practice is part of the process in relation to equipping people with tools to empower them. Knowledge sits as part of a power structure in psychotherapy, and teaching people practices and techniques is a form of gifting the power to the other. Manualised practices are subject to time structures and need adaptation as they can be too rigid.

Therapist 4 – 'Making Sense'

Psychotherapy takes multiple positioning points from varying theoretical foundations, all of which are situated in a context within a community of practice and should be acknowledged as so. Manualised approaches such as cognitive behavioural therapy (CBT) can feel disconnected due to their starting point and lack of flexibility to adapt in relation to need. There is a central focus on being human in the therapeutic relationship before any theoretical understanding of what is occurring, therefore being oneself as a therapist is part of the process. Phenomenological lens allows the therapist an avenue by which he feels he can be with the client in an authentic way and as such there is an aliveness as client and therapist are open to creating new understandings which permit a redefining of meaning through new ideas relevant to the individuality of each person. Being human in the room models authenticity and encourages an encounter that belongs to the individual involved. Highly manualised practice can be difficult to compute and arbitrary if restrictions and regulations have no foundational understanding.

Therapist 5 – 'Breaking the Flow'

The therapist describes manualised interventions as breaking the flow of therapy and shutting down connectivity with the self and the other. There is a cutting off from the self that takes place which lends itself to producing outcomes rather than a being with. The disconnection is from the whole and the bigger picture is problematic as the therapy and sense of self can become lost in the detail. When highly manualised, there is a restriction to the client's freedom described and a sense of withdrawal from the therapy. Manualised interventions do not feel anchored and instead sit in the head space which can limit a fuller experience available. Manualised practices are derived from external sources and start in the wrong position as they are not grounded in the therapeutic encounter. Tools and techniques from manualised practice can be creative, educational, protective, and helpful when not restrictive. They can be used by clients and therapists in the moment but only if led by the session as opposed to the session leading the practice. Highly manualised practice impacts the ability to attend to clients and support them on their journey to find themselves and be whole. Whilst the tools and techniques can be useful to help people arrive in the room and begin the work, psychotherapy is a diverse and multilayered encounter which incorporates all aspects of the client. Manualised approaches such as CBT can get in the way of a deep meaningful and nuanced connection. When used as a set intervention with no flexibility, it can hinder the liberating, creative, and impromptu nature of therapy which is practice led rather than theory led. The mathematical nature of CBT positions itself in a right and wrong binary that then causes confusion due to the volume of information and prioritising thinking over experience. Focus is on the goal rather than the moment, and the agenda is designed to fulfil external pressures. The person disappears when there is a sole focus on the symptom and not the whole. Conflicted when feeling morally responsible and having to disregard something that is in the room because it does not fit the model. Tools are better used as experimental in the space between client and therapist than as set interventions with a move towards authenticity rather than a goal.

Therapist 6 – 'Being and Bravery'

In psychotherapy there is more space to travel in different directions and explore in more natural ways but that there is an element of bravery involved because you are reliant on yourself as the resource. There is a sense of bravery and courage to carry out therapy which is not structured and planned out session by session. The therapist needs to be able to cope with a certain degree of messiness and chaos that is unresolved as part of the process. Levels of bravery have changed over the years due to working in more prescribed environments such as the NHS. Not knowing where a situation or conversation is going can be scary because you're reliant on your own being. Experience of non-manualised approaches is a sense of herself being in the room with the other. Bravery is orientated around trusting herself and feeling that when she brings herself to the sessions it's enough. Caught in evidence chasing but as time went on, she started to realise she could offer something of high value herself. It is less about freedom and more about being able to use all of herself and knowledge to respond. Responsiveness is what feels important. The experience of being audited in a person-centred capacity during a clinical trial meant it lost its heart.

Therapist 7 – 'Faith and Trust Leads to Magic and Gold Dust'

Manualised tools and techniques have a utility to them and can be helpful in moments of 'stuckness' or to experiment with ideas and experiences in a creative manner. The tools and techniques are geared towards arriving at a connective place rather than to achieve an outcome. There is a focus on the inner world being accessed, and techniques and tools can work alongside being with the client if they are helpful and relevant to the client in the moment. Highly manualised interventions feel unhelpful as there is a magic that occurs in therapy which springs from the unexpected. There is an adventurous aspect to therapy in which she follows the energy of the client and trusts they are moving towards something authentic and helpful. Meeting clients in this place and connecting with them can feel like gold dust as they meet the client during a moment of discovery within themselves. Although there is still a loose sense of how the session might progress or where it might move towards, the therapist considers it important that an agenda does not take over as it hinders being truly present with the client. The focus is less about results and answers and more about trusting the process and having faith that the quality of the relationship can be a process of change in itself. There is a belief and confidence in allowing the therapy to unfold rather than needing to know what the next steps are. Organisational needs of services can have limitations on the time scale the therapist has, having a negative impact on these processes being able to flourish and close in a good place.

Therapist 8 – 'Giving Space to Accept and Being Oneself'

They became a therapist through a combination of factors which were both personal and natural qualities such as wanting to help others and empathy. They see the role with clients as a facilitator of a space from which the client can grow in their own way. To use this space up with an agenda has felt alien to the therapist and rarely has the planning of manualised interventions materialised with clients causing a deviation from the model back to a practice the therapist has faith in. Whilst having understood what is required of her to pass the criteria set by training, she has had to adapt the practice due to a clash of values. Leading sessions is not how the therapist would like to practice but instead feels a combination of approaches as the most helpful to prepare her for therapeutic encounters. Her marker of a good session is the connectivity with the client and the authenticity in the room which, she feels, comes from a sense of feeling understood and accepted. By giving space for clients to be there as a normalising of the self rather than thinking there is something wrong with them that they need to fix. Whilst the therapist appreciates that too much space can be overwhelming for people, too much technical intervention can feel like a pressure to 'fix' people. When space is offered, the client can invite her to go to deeper levels, but interventions led by her often stay surface level. It is the space given that leads to connectivity and an openness from clients. She describes the difference as head and heart, stating that a more embodied and full experience feels like heart and techniques more in the realm of the head.

Therapist 9 – 'Protective Layer'

The therapist experiences manualised practice as a different state of mind in which there are rules, bureaucracy, measurement, and management. Whilst seeing the benefits for early interventions, manualised treatments serve as a protective layer against risky and the overwhelming need of clients. She describes these interventions as contained but one which serves the therapist as they control the agenda. The experience is one of being 'up against the clock' and pressured. There is a sense of pressure to perform and produce for clients and the organisation. She speaks about a punitive experience both for her and for the clients if the work is not carried out. Facing risks of complaints, the therapist must justify and prove her interventions to the team and management; this in turn can lead to pushing clients away. Describing it as a formula, manualised approaches like CBT hold the agenda and are therapist-led, although it's not about the therapist. She experiences the demands of being a therapist before she enters the room due to the quantity of things that need to be thought about. Being a therapist is a particular identity she prepares for and moves into before sessions.

Therapist 10 – 'Personal Growth'

Highly manualised practice is a missed opportunity to offer deep authentic therapy. There is a high value to spaces which offer possibility, connection, and creativity to flourish with new emerging discoveries. Therapy is a calling for him, and he speaks of being lucky enough to combine his creative practices with his work. Manualised practice simplifies the human experience for him and removes individuality of both himself and the client causing frustrations which are also experienced and fed back by the clients. The therapist describes his experience of theories such as existentialism and philosophy as broad concepts which are more helpful to both practice and people. But he describes specific models within CBT as a specific skill that has a low level of application in its usefulness.

There is a two-way process experienced from which the therapist learns from the clients they encounter. He describes how clients might say something that resonates with his past personal experience and how this offers him an opportunity of growth. The relationship is described as an equal one in which both client and therapist can gain insights and self-reflections. The therapist describes a feeling of liberation when entering private practice because he could work with the client's agenda and simply work on being a good therapist. He describes institutions and models as having their agendas on how people should deliver therapy. His move to private practice is described as no longer governed by institutions or money to some degree.

Therapist 11 – 'Moving with a Still Heart'

Therapeutic encounters should be and are, for the therapist, centred around 'being' rather than thinking which she describes as being led by a 'still heart'. There is a sense of spirituality that runs through being with another person in a way that connects and meets them where they are. Manualised practices push the therapist into thinking mode where there is a sense of busyness and a push to fulfil an agenda. Techniques and manualised tools are seen as aids which are banked over time and which can be withdrawn when needed in order that a client can speak of where they are. Thinking with the head and feeling with the heart are vastly different places for the therapist, and not feeling centred results in a defensiveness within her. Her state of being changes as she tries to hit a marker, rather than a natural intuition which emerges in the still heart zone. There is a moving together through connectedness and attunement on an implicit level which is nourishing and where things naturally fall into the space rather than a manualised approach which feels disconnected and forced.

Therapist 12 – 'Witnessing and Being with – Breathe Them in'

Tools and techniques are helpful for clients to find a connection to themselves and move towards authenticity in their experience. For the therapist, the purpose is for clients to feel witnessed in their authentic selves so that they may work it through whilst feeling connected to another. There is an intuition and a confidence in knowing how to be with a client and allow whatever they bring to emerge. Described as a deeper level of knowing which is not cognitive, the therapist describes an air between them that is created and to be able to breathe them in. Manualised interventions can move that space and reshape it in a way that does not feel authentic. Tools and techniques can be creative and experimental to help open something up for the client, but the client must come first and feel ready.

Broader Emerging Themes from Therapist Conversations

There are eight key topics which have emerged from the research findings and which best articulate areas most relevant to the book. It is not uncommon that the key points might at times overlap as there are often interrelated conversations. For example, feelings of 'authenticity' might be discussed in relation to experiences of validation and audit culture, whilst still being discussed independently of each other. Each theme offers an account taken from all the interviews in combination. Words which are in italic are representative of particular words and statements which emerged and stand out as descriptors used.

Personal Histories

Every therapist spoke of entering the profession of psychotherapy either with a history of helping others or needing help themselves. They described how their experiences feel entwined with their work not simply through their framework but through their interests in practice. Their selection of training often aligns with their experiences and how they want to show up in the world. Each therapist has a personal story relating to their journey in becoming therapists. There is a personal affiliation with the way therapists practise which they describe as deeper than producing outcomes. For some, they articulated how it is a form of identity for them.

Reflections were given from three therapists of their journey from a point of crisis to becoming a therapist. This transformation involved seeking help, going through therapy, and ultimately '*finding purpose in helping others*'. Painful pasts were highlighted across the interviews as therapists shared their personal difficulties and how these experiences sparked a fascination with the psychological workings of people. Described was an acute sense of difficulty with interventions that dismissed or made them feel cut off from the work. Some would talk of their values being compromised and a conflict with what was being asked of them when carrying out CBT tasks.

Many of the therapists interviewed felt there was a great deal to be gained not only by having their own experience of therapy as a point of reference but also for working through their own difficulties. A sense of togetherness and connectivity through experience and empathy was described as an '*openness*' to help and support. Therapists talked about continuing their journeys by developing and growing from their encounters with clients. They could learn from the client as much as they could support. In particular, the importance of relational depth was mentioned numerous times and described as connective and embodied.

Within the interviews, the therapists would speak of their preferred practice or way of being with clients. They articulated learning through their own practice but often hindered by restrictions to their sense of self when pushed into rigid manualised interventions. Every therapist brought their story to the interview as a motivator towards their desire to become a therapist. Some described a '*deep calling*', others felt '*saved by therapy*' articulating how they knew what psychotherapy was capable of and the potential behind therapy. In every case whilst there was an appreciation for structured interventions, every therapist preferred a relational, fluid, and dynamic approach to being with clients. The relational and structured appeared as therapists described some of the inherent qualities they experienced when moving away from a manualised approach. They also described a feeling of independence, establishing a relationship with themselves and the '*freedom to practise and learn what matters*'. Several adopted a phenomenological lens as a preference for a specific mode of inquiry and understanding. They articulated their surprise at '*how brave*' they had to become and how they learnt to cope better with the messiness of experience. One therapist described how the NHS is so prescribed that people don't have venture into the '*big scary stuff*'. Another therapist described their journey through different therapeutic approaches, such as person-centred therapy and Gestalt therapy. They expressed a preference for the latter, emphasising its assertiveness and holistic perspective. Throughout all the interview, there was a preference for integrating new models of thought into practice for personal development.

The Need for Adaption in Manualised Practice

The theme of adapting manualised interventions was paramount throughout. Each therapist found a way to adapt highly manualised practices. They described having to '*get around certain restrictions secretly*' in order that they could help their clients. Several therapists felt they were not supposed to be adapting the model as it would mean coming off track. In several cases, there felt a risk in doing so and a fear of being reprimanded by management or a supervisor. Attempts were repeatedly made to add more sessions or skip parts so that the client could freely talk about what was going on for them. In many cases there needed to be '*a justification or a case put forward for extra sessions*'. NHS environments were described as highly audited and how every intervention needed to be approved and any changes or deviations from the treatment plan needed to be explained to management. If the client came off track by '*speaking about anything outside of the remit of the manualised intervention*' or scores were significantly different, the treatment model could not be changed and as such the client would need to go on a new waiting list for a separate treatment to manage the new behaviour or risk level. This was described as '*awful to see*' as the therapist knew they would be waiting a long time. They described an '*ethical struggle*' with a system which '*felt was punitive to high-risk clients*'. What felt particularly difficult was that the therapist was qualified and could see this client if they allowed her to. This was not granted, and her capacity as a psychotherapist was limited to manualised interventions because of the protocol in place. The sense of not using the therapist fully appeared in many of the interviews as therapists gave descriptions of '*holding back*' and not having enough time to unpack something else with the client. However, challenges were faced within school settings, including the evolving expectations, the pressure to adopt a more medical model, and the difficulty of addressing emerging mental health issues in students.

Time limitations repeatedly came into the conversations as therapists described how they needed '*space for encounters of resonating and connectedness to emerge*' stating that each client is different and there is no time scale for when these moments can happen. Impact to the depth of therapy was spoken of as '*short-term work stays surface level rather than opening possibilities*' for the client. Without the space to allow this work to unfold, the therapist stays in a safe place offering skills to manage what is on the surface.

The practice gap was referred to as therapists explored the difficulties of the real-world application of highly manualised interventions. Therapists experienced a gap with academic research and interventions not accounting for the resources available to them. They felt that interventions were designed under ideal conditions which '*fail to account for the rarity of ideal conditions in practice*' or that '*sessions are normally evening work in a venue that is in the middle of nowhere*'. Other factors included the difficulty faced with clients wanting to address other situations or enter a conversation that had not been planned for. The lack of space afforded for these conversations was felt to have a negative impact on the therapeutic relationship as they spoke of '*feeling disconnected*' from their clients. In addition, resources were experienced as a major impingement on practice being carried out. Manualised interventions which had been created and showed high levels of efficacy in the test phase did not play out in the same way when attempts were made to apply the model. Often therapists spoke of there not being the same resources, time, or equipment to fulfil the intervention. This often resulted in therapists drawing on their own resources. Some of the new therapists struggled and felt out of their depth.

Intuitive timing presented itself in different ways throughout the interviews. All interviewees made mention of different needs at different times and that sometimes there are unexpected changes that take place in life which alter what a client needs in the moment. They described rigid interventions as not responsive in the moment. Therapists described a felt sense of when to try a tool or technique with a client and how certain techniques could aid the client in moving through '*stuckness*' or to help '*open up thinking and reflection*' on a specific issue. Here techniques were described as helpful and '*part of a tool kit*'. There is value placed on approaches which are grounded in principles or attitudes and which could be considered a structured or manualised approaches.

Some therapist struggled when forced to continue with steps and protocols despite the clients need to express something different or come away from the agenda to some degree. They described difficulties with '*authenticity and connectivity as relationships can take time to build and create a safe space for clients to start reaching relational depth*'.

All therapists expressed a desire for freedom to use the techniques in a way that is adapted to that person, fitting in with understanding them and what they want from therapy. But this '*freedom comes from having space and time to build the trust*'. A discussion is had with instances where certain techniques may not work or might evoke resistance in clients. This finds balance of commitment to understanding the client's needs and goals, but that often there would be instances where clients may come in with a '*fix me mentality*'. They discuss the importance of finding a balance between providing techniques and understanding the underlying issues contributing to the challenges clients face.

Adaption felt relevant for the '*real-world application*' and to try and maintain psychotherapy as a holistic practice. This was described as a knowledge which is embodied rather than a fact held as a logic. Some spoke of never having seen a manualised model followed without some form of personal adaption on the part of the practitioner. Direct links were made to CBT, DBT, and systemic therapy as examples of where deviations have taken place. Again, the theme of embodiment is discussed further as a separate theme but for this theme the relevance is about the other ways of knowing through and with the body as a '*deeper level of knowing*'.

The idea of knowledge returned several times as a conversation of how we can know in different ways. What is articulated here is a holistic approach as well as embodied form of knowledge as previously mentioned. How learning came from the client especially from asking '*how are they participating and responding to communication in the world?*'. Knowledge was described as an '*ongoing lesson*' and often comes from being able to '*converse with otherness in some form*'.

Whilst training prepared therapists in some way, several spoke about feeling they could '*relax and adapt the models*' after their training had finished. With some saying, '*they no longer follow the protocol*'. Others talked about never believing in what they were doing when training in manualised interventions but needed to finish the course. Therapists spoke of '*enjoyment of learning despite occasional discomfort or feelings of being an imposter*'. Again, there is a freedom to develop but that there is still a restriction to thinking differently in the NHS.

Experiences of 'Authenticity'

As the findings were brought together, therapists repeatedly spoke about their sense of authenticity being impacted by high demands from organisations. This showed up in several ways. Agenda proved to be significantly difficult when not driven by the client. Conflicts of pre-designed agendas which did not consider the current situation for the clients and therapeutic relationship were seen as problematic. Timing was entwined with intuition, and this was an essential part of connectedness. Therefore, timing played a crucial role in authenticity which gives '*unfolding*' and creative speech a central stage. As such, therapists preferred that clients could speak their own truths if it felt appropriate. Tools and techniques served best when promoting more speech. As such the tools often orientated around expression, moving through '*stuckness*', offering words as descriptors. Therapists described the impact felt on the sense of authenticity when in a pre-planned session rather than in the moment. Timing was linked to authenticity, and a '*not knowing what will be said next*' felt different to prescribed questions.

Therapists emphasised the importance of authenticity in navigating challenges and changes, speaking of the importance to providing '*culturally relevant therapy*', wanting to have a commitment to authenticity in understanding and addressing clients' diverse backgrounds and experiences. Exploring connectivity with the self is also considered in relation to authenticity. Therapists described it as feeling '*hard*' to try to help some connect with themselves if they themselves were not connected.

Constraints and limitations of manualised therapy were experienced as discomfort with the '*lack of flexibility*'. They describe feeling challenged by manualised person-centred work and the struggle to maintain authenticity within a structured framework. Personal struggle and impact on well-being was discussed in relation to '*being pulled away*' from their authentic self.

This affected their well-being and satisfaction. Connection to self resulted in a conversation about lived experience and how those feed into understanding and practice. All participants have predominantly come from a place of experience when entering the work.

The conversation of connecting and being responsive to the client felt paramount in articulating the need to be present in the room and adapt to the situation. They described the work as a '*responsiveness and helping people return and connect to themselves*'. But also, that they too are on a journey of growth and development and that they at times need to connect with the other. The relationship to technique and tools was described as '*knowing when and how to use tools and techniques to help facilitate this connection*'. There is a need for each individual to understand each situation and to understand the parameters ahead of time. There is a struggle to get on board with ideas or concepts that are not in some way logical or helpful. Understanding can be developed not only through past and present experiences but also through logic and research, and therefore, therapists spoke of being '*open to new theoretical ideas if they make sense*'.

Internal and External Validation of Practice

Throughout the interviews, therapists seem to allocate blame to themselves or doubt when they felt they could not carry out the full manualised intervention. On several occasions the therapist would talk about '*not being skilled enough*' and this is why they must adapt the intervention. They rarely allocated any of their difficulties to the intervention whilst simultaneously talking about how the real-world application is not good. Descriptors such as '*not knowing enough*' or '*not being experienced enough*' are used despite having experience, qualifications and training. Several therapists talked about how they felt other therapists did not have similar problems and that the intervention potentially failed because of their lack.

Often the sheer number of interventions available in manualised practice left the therapist feeling they were behind or uninformed on the latest update and how this contributed towards a lack of confidence. One therapist commented on '*feeling isolated in practice*' and that there is a lack of sharing experiences and a mistrust in training institutions which do not give voice to diversity of thought. They spoke of trying to find community outside of the core traditional training programmes to independent organisations such as 'The Black, African and Asian Therapy Network' (BAATN) which privileges the embodied inner experiences of therapists and integrates these voices into mainstream psychology. Other therapists talked of not wanting to tell others that they were struggling and found it difficult to share experiences. Opportunities to discuss opposing views were often shut down in manualised training which caused therapists to either find an alternate community or stop challenging.

For some practitioners their development over time helped with feelings of validation and as such they were able to practise in a more relaxed and integrated manner. Practitioners spoke about their confidence building after gaining experience through practice. In direct relation to manualised practice, therapist described becoming better towards the requirements over time as they integrated their counselling skills and developed trust in the practice. Initial experience was one of feeling squeezed and oppressed by manualised forms of practice but that this did become easier as they became more proficient.

For other participants there was a questioning on their own ability to provide interventions properly because they had only just qualified. There was an acknowledgement of issues with manualised interventions whilst simultaneously questioning if they were perhaps '*not well versed*' enough as a reason for the practices being such a challenge to them. For another participant, their ability to deliver interventions also developed but the experience did not change, instead it can become more difficult over time because they felt '*cut off*' in sessions. There was a '*lack of grounding or anchoring throughout*' in manualised practice.

In manualised practice, participants felt they came away from their '*embodied sense of the space and more into a thinking space*'. This is in relation to all the modalities not just CBT, the context is that some of the therapies must emerge in the moment, and therefore, practice can feel restrictive if prescribed beforehand and not responsive in the moment.

Training, Learning, and Developing

Therapists when exploring their own experiences articulated several ways in which they develop. They described '*leaning towards praxis*' as therapists felt they could learn not only from their conversations with clients but from their explorations in supervision, peer, and platforms that felt personal to them. Training came up inadvertently when the researcher asked the therapists what informs them. Several of the therapists spoke of learning from their clients and practise whilst others referred to workshops and direct training for development. Supervision and peer support also came through as a learning practice with therapists saying they enjoy '*a diverse network of learning*' and how this encourages them.

Brought into discussion was the 'recruit to train' programs provided by the National Health Service England (NHSE) as part of the IAPT services which are on the rise in the United Kingdom and aimed at expanding the workforce. These programs actively embed 'evidence-based practice' into organisations and are geared around maximising the output of CBT and short-term interventions. Three of the therapists interviewed in this research, completed training with IAPT, and, whilst they found it very informative, described high levels of anxiety and an erosion of their confidence. They often reverted to their counselling training when the manualised practices did not translate. They all described the difficulties in applying what was being taught and one therapist described training videos having scripted clients to demonstrate the models. The therapist found it confusing that the demonstrations did not use real clients and that the '*scripts felt unrealistic on what went on in the therapy room*'. Therapists described how training did not always take on contextual understandings. Whilst another therapist felt very lucky that their training had prepared them for understanding how '*organisations impact on practice*', they described this learning module as helpful because they never anticipated this issue but later this became needed when working for charities and the NHS.

Therapists spoke of a preference for communal shared learning which, they feel, promotes self-discovery, rather than training which was '*increasingly content heavy and very much teacher led*'. Therapists described being with others as an essential core practice for them. Training which incorporated elements of experiential learning and personal engagement from therapists also offered them a baseline for being with others in a way that could leave them open to learning from their clients. Therapists described manualised practice missing this component, stating that whilst this can be taught in theory, the practice of such an endeavour must be experienced.

What emerged was a duality, therapists wanted knowledge in the form of techniques and theories which they could use as tools in therapy. As a desire to build their '*tool belt*' therapists wanted to feel equipped to be in the room with clients. Across the board there was an appreciation for methods and techniques; however, therapists experience a move from using the techniques to being used by the techniques. They felt manualised techniques were at their best when they could be adapted. Therapists described needing to get a '*felt sense and context-specific understanding*', to know how to respond.

As some therapists discussed a sense of readiness to train, life experiences came up as a doubt for them taking on psychotherapeutic training. Some therapists felt they had not encountered enough in their lives to warrant becoming a therapist which they felt had implications for their sense of validation and confidence in the room. Training was seen as a practice ground with theoretical understanding of what is going on rather than simply a teaching of technics.

This sense of depersonalisation and lack of '*personal twist*' impeded engagement and created an environment of '*staleness*'. With a lack of diversity in thought and training, therapists described a hunger for open dialogue and a telling of '*experiences rather than a telling of theory*'. Often this could lead therapists to disengage or shut down due to a lack of personal affiliation. They described a frustration towards uncritical admiration of historical figures, particularly Sigmund Freud, and spoke of a need to '*acknowledge both positive and negative aspects of these figures*'. They share their disappointment with encountering prejudice and stereotypes within the field of therapy and training. They express a desire for more open-mindedness and less discrimination, experiencing how academic individuals can sometimes exhibit more prejudice and how knowledge can be used to reinforce pre-existing beliefs. Therapists discussed some of the challenges they faced during their training, particularly when their approach clashed with the training requirements, leading to stress. They also highlight the impact of being observed through video recording and how this hindered their ability to be present in the moment during therapy sessions. These types of practices were described as '*arbitrary*' and considered distracting.

Power dynamics became increasingly prevalent in the interviews with references to dynamics in education and training, on an organisational level and within the therapeutic relationship itself. The conversations touched on the stressors faced in training, especially those trained in manualised approaches, and the need for more comprehensive training and supervision, speaking of how they learn and develop in their practice. Beneficial to one therapist was training components that could contextualise and assist in understanding the implications of organisational structures in the workplace. They felt this to be not only helpful in bringing to light the issues faced but also practical in how to best try to manage this with practice.

Culture of Auditing and Administration in NHS Services

Work environments had a fundamental impact on the experience of therapists in their practice. Interviewees spoke of the way work setting and practices could and did influence a therapist's decision-making when it came to where they wanted to work. Several of the therapists described leaving organisations to move into private practice where there would be '*more freedom to practice in creative ways*'. Therapists described seeing colleagues around them struggle with restrictive practices and witnessed '*peers suffer in similar roles when the work environment has been so demanding*', directly stating that they felt able to stay in the organisation because they had not '*become like that yet*'. The therapist was describing how other peers felt in the NHS and how this was one of the most demanding and restrictive of environments. Another therapist who works in the NHS said it can often feel '*punitive and inflexible in its systematic approach to care*'.

Experiences of pressures from different systems at play such as organisational, political, and financial all have had an impact but the therapist spoke of not wavering from their therapeutic practice without a justifiable reason, whilst others felt they had no choice. For the therapist, moving away towards a rule following system without questioning risks the danger of '*dehumanising the process and impeding a growth*' through consistently defining meaning.

Several conversations were had regarding the comparison between NHS and Charity/Private Sector Work, describing their experience of working in the NHS and how it compares to their current role in a charity and private practice. They spoke of '*satisfying experiences in counselling*' and emphasised for them the importance of organisational support and the balance between freedom and boundaries which feel more restrictive in the NHS.

Other therapists described a revolving door effect in the NHS as the management tried to be more cost-effective but how this backfired as clients consistently keeping coming back. One therapist in the NHS spoke about manualised practices becoming '*a protective layer towards the caseloads and levels of complexity*' in the work. They described a service which was in such high demand that they needed not to be fully open and encounter clients at such relational depth. This would become too difficult to cope with given the level of need experienced and workload. The importance of knowing limitation came up for therapists to not put a power dynamic onto the client of an all-seeing and all-being all-wondrous therapists. Manualised interventions could be used as a protective layer for the exposure to '*high-risk, highly complex clients and large caseload*'. The combination of all three factors felt overwhelming for the therapist, and as such, having restrictive practices enabled a layer between them and '*all the needs of clients*'.

Caseloads, '*administrative burden*', and insufficient support were highlighted in relation to high levels of manualised interventions, alongside increased levels of preparation and constantly trying to keep up with where each client was in the process to stay on track. The caseload of the therapist often hindered the capacity to engage on a deep and meaningful level which they are trained to do but instead must remain to some degree detached for their own well-being. Similar conversations emerged with other therapists regarding the challenges faced particularly in the NHS Talking Therapies world. Therapists spoke of struggles and frustration with work when administrative tasks limit the '*ability to engage in the more relational, person-centred aspects of counselling*'. In addition, there is little interaction on a relational level with supervisory support as some therapists were managed by non-clinicians and had limited time with clinical supervisors and peer support.

In heavily monitored institutions, therapists feared repercussions if interventions were not working or targets were not met. Training was also a significant factor as therapists often would do what was needed to pass the course and then start to adapt their practice afterwards. There was a sense that the training often felt unrealistic and '*difficult to replicate in the real world*' as conditions would not be ideal. Therapists described experiences of cutting off clients because it did not meet the agenda, and although '*it felt wrong*', therapists would continue because they were being monitored for assessment. There are several examples within the findings which show a tension between following protocol and adapting to the situation.

A core concern emerging from the interviews across all 12 was in relation to manualised interventions being leading for both client and therapist. There was a consensus with every therapist that bringing in a rigid agenda from start to finish felt limiting and against their sense of being. Difficulty with agendas derived from outside the therapy room showed to be a core concern '*due to the lack of understanding*' and other times a power imbalance was felt in dictating how the sessions would go. Highly manualised frameworks and agendas proved difficult for each therapist in their own way. Some therapists moved modalities to a more open and person-centred foundation if they had the ability to do so but still acknowledging it can fall under the manualised remit. They adopted a more phenomenological inquiry approach as part of the foundation to their work.

Therapists found it challenging and disconnected to their sense of logic at times as interventions felt '*like checklists without reason or a deeper understanding*' of why something is being asked, often feeling '*out of context and arbitrary*'. Some therapists struggled with organisational pressures which hindered practice as short-term work was the only possible support to offer clients. Pressures to the organisational funding often could be felt by the therapists as resources diminished, with modality thresholds used to prioritised access. This was picked up in the interviews with a therapist discussing their frustration at institutions and models of practice being restrictive for the therapist and clients. They also described frustration at feeling unable to adapt the model due to organisational pressures.

Others pointed to the time spend and lost when interventions are disconnected from the client themselves. Interventions would be planned but become irrelevant in the room as clients would '*arrive in ways which the model could not anticipate*'. The reality of how clients show up rarely matched the expectations of the intervention. Although person-centred, therapists often would have to shut down what a client wanted to discuss so that the intervention could be delivered in the timeframe. Therapists also described frustrations with a system that allows people to tap out and not have to engage with their process if they don't like the formula.

This sentiment is also reflected by therapists articulating the challenges and bravery required in counselling, acknowledging a shift from a more courageous approach to a more structured one, especially in their current NHS role. They would feel better when able to respond to the client with all their training rather than being restricted to a model. Their freedom to practice became and remains a central factor when thinking of where they want to work. This aligned with another therapist's account of feeling that their psychoanalytic training was not being used but available and always informing them even if they can't respond with it.

A therapist supervisor talked through their experiences of trying to help their supervisees navigate the constraints and restrictions of manualised interventions, especially when they have no other background to fall on. Discussions emerged in relation to only training in manualised practice and how this left the therapist ill equipped at times to manage what was emerging in the room if not in a manual.

Flexibility repeatedly stood out as an important factor and there being space for the therapist to incorporate techniques based on what resonates with the client. It feels important to let the session get lost to some degree without fear. Describing a balance between providing psychoeducation and implementing techniques, '*whilst considering the preferences and needs of the clients*'. Just being with the client and '*holding their experience*' in mind can be beneficial. That there is not always a need for an agenda unless the client is feeling nervous without one. Several therapists struggled with the idea of controlling the agenda. They felt their values and ethics were compromised, particularly during training to deliver specific interventions. Highlighting the need to be client led and that the therapy is a two-way process which allows the client to *'become the driver of the therapy'*.

Therapists talked about things getting missed because there is a strong focus on the narrow margins provided by highly manualised practices and how they can get in the way of contextual understanding or even simply being able to follow a lead with the client. They spoke of their dissatisfaction and frustration with solely delivering interventions which '*does not reflect human experience in the world*'. They articulated how it does not offer clients any preparation to deal with issues in the outside world as the scope is too '*narrow and safe*'. It does not prepare them from the unexpected and does not reflect how relationships work within such a narrow scope. There is a fear that something can be missed as the therapist speaks about being highly focussed on specifics. There needs to be '*a sense of the bigger picture*' that can encompass more of what is going and how non-manualised approaches allow them to show up feeling '*more present and fuller*'.

Again, when discussing high levels of manualised practice, it does not necessarily mean CBT as this modality is not always highly manualised. One therapist describes their taking part in randomised controlled trials that were aimed at providing a manualised version of person-centred approaches; however, the therapist found this to have a similar impact to other manualised interventions. There was a struggle with being audited against a standard and how this felt false and unrealistic because '*the situation was false*'. Focus was too centralised on meeting the target rather than being with the client.

They speak of the hindering process which takes place and the lack of development under certain conditions. That often there can feel an emptiness and a lack of space for someone's evolution in therapy. Space for nuance or exploring is limited unlike psychodynamic practices which feel more humane and organic. They speak of their evolution in therapeutic style and how they have moved away from a reliance on specific techniques and models. They emphasise the '*importance of being attuned to the client's needs and allowing sessions to unfold naturally*'. Some therapists found it disruptive to have clients switch over to other therapists because they no longer meet the criteria of being in a particular intervention. The burden to clients can be traumatic, especially if they know they are being moved around in relation to what is being said in the room.

This linked in with other conversations about '*justice and equity in access to mental health services*' and touches on the potential systemic limitations and challenges in providing comprehensive care. This therapist related it to the medical model in which the client is set into a position which begins from the viewpoint that they are in some way sick and require treatment and to be triaged but that psychotherapy resists being with a client in a medicalised way.

The experience of being audited surfaced several times when attempting to carry out a person-centred manualised approach and described as going against their way of being. They found themselves thinking about the delivery of the model rather than being. Several times it is mentioned about having a foundation to work from and how manualised practice can add and be integrated.

Embodied Experiences

The findings articulated that therapists experienced a sense of being cut off from the body and a lack of '*wholeness*' in highly manualised interventions. Comments such as '*being cut off from the waist*' and being stuck in a '*head space*' were used to describe how they felt restricted in their practice as procedural processes shaped how they engaged with the other. They talked about the ways manualised interventions impacted the ability to make use of their full selves.

A core theme that was described throughout the interviews and which appeared highly relevant was the impact on connectivity with varying levels of manualised interventions. Whilst tools and techniques chosen in session and introduced by either the therapist or the client appeared as '*helpful and experimental*', manualised interventions that were pre-designed from beginning to end were seen much less favourable as they were deemed to '*have a negative impact in the room*'. A disconnect occurred in three primary domains, connection and relational depth with the client, connection to self, and a lack of authenticity in the room.

This aspect of connectivity appeared within different terminologies but with the same connotations to it. Therapists spoke about a sense of being with the client, meeting the client in relational depth, absorbing, and witnessing. That '*being with*' the client whilst they are in difficulty feels a valuable part of the process. The connectivity is also described as breathing in the space between client and therapist and having intuition and confidence about knowing how to be with a client. Therapists also spoke about being able to hold what a client brings and allowing for them to recognise what they need to do for themselves. This sense of connectivity showed itself to also be a gauge of the success of a session being felt. Therapists state how they could sense a good session not because of a metric but because there was a deep attunment and connection.

This aligns with connectivity as the therapist describes moments in therapy where there's a sense of magic or flow, emphasising the connection between therapist and client. They express a preference for allowing sessions to evolve organically rather than adhering strictly to a planned agenda. This was similar in the previous themes when building the relationship as therapists stated that the relationship was the treatment.

The sense of being absorbed was an embodied experience for therapists. That a form of emotional or psychological connectivity in the therapeutic relationship could emerge when letting the client lead rather than bringing in an intervention. That being fully present with the client is at the heart of connectivity. On several occasions the comment of being human and present with the client came up, suggesting that being fully present is crucial for establishing a meaningful connectivity with another person. They stated that the best results come from a client feeling like they are talking to another human and the consequences of not fully showing up.

Descriptions often spoke of an experience of aliveness within the space when they meet their clients at a relational depth. This aliveness could feel both positive and challenging at different times. Both the darker and brighter moments could be experienced with such deep richness in the therapeutic process, using the metaphor of climbing a mountain and navigating a dark forest to represent the challenges faced by clients in therapy. The therapist expresses confidence gained from personal experiences, having been through their own "dark forest", and believes in the possibility of finding a path through challenges. They spoke of an internal validation and a faith in the process, highlighting the fluid, felt, and changing nature of therapy which requires the therapist to move with if they want to be with. Conversations about attunement emerged when trying to reach a place where meaningful connections and self-discovery occur. This attunement and the depth of the relationship is crucial in the process. An emphasis is placed on the time and space this can take in therapy to achieve these moments and how organisational needs and manuals limit and hinder these experiences. Through using too many tools, a sense of contact and presence is lost with the client, again leading to experiences that the session did not feel right for the therapist.

This challenge of balancing technique with attunement and personal connection can also incorporate creative techniques, like metaphors, art, and music to facilitate conversations, especially in trauma work. These feel to be useful in attuning to clients' energy and body language and creating a safe space for them to explore freely and in their own time. They do not work well when forced or part of an entire manual process.

Energy in the room is discussed through changes in the body language but also as *a 'primary source of knowing'* if there is a connection and what the therapist might be connecting to. Techniques in this sense are geared towards opening '*conversations and encouraging engagement*' on the part of the client. This engagement in relation to the interviews is shown through speech, depth of emotion, or expression predominantly in the therapeutic space.

They describe a view of therapy as different to a medicalised way of being with clients. Instead, they spoke of the ability to love and see people beyond their symptoms and to '*encounter clients as a human being*', to remain within professional boundaries but that the therapist '*makes contact with the essence of the human and to bring it forward*'.

They also described an embodied self and how this feels different between psychotherapy and CBT practices. In psychotherapy there is an awareness of breathing, heaviness, sadness, agitation, or even arousal as examples. In CBT that is dampened and so physicality shows up more dominantly. They can feel their arm on the desk, the pen in their hand, and cramping from the pencil as they write. They can feel rumbles from hunger or a full blader and describes this as coming from disengagement with an existential perspective, saying '*the body steps in and the scales tip*'.

One therapist compared CBT to physiotherapy saying that if someone has a bad hip they go to a physiotherapist and they won't really see the person, but they will see the hip, and they'll give things to do for the hip. CBT is the mental health version, but it means '*people don't get seen as people*'. The condition is seen before anything else. In addition, a lack of flexibility meant clients needed to fit into a disorder and how they had to work with the idea that they had this disorder rather than helping them explore the narrative of their life; it could often feel dismissive of the client.

Embodiment was key throughout the interviews and conversations of the full body experience. The body was spoken of in relation to feeling cut off in parts; therapists described manualised interventions as feeling *"cut off from the neck"*. Therapists described how they feel they don't exist in the room when following restrictive procedures and their fear that the clients also don't feel any sense of aliveness from the rigid protocols.

Four therapists spoke about experiential learning for themselves and learning through the body. This also ties into a sense of embodiment in learning. Embodiment showed up as unquantifiable but the desire to explore how experiences in the room had an impact felt very present in learning about the self and the other. Throughout the interviews there is a reference to the body being able to absorb, tap into, and understand a different form of knowledge. The body gives the sensation of lending itself over to the other, described by one therapist as being fully there when speaking about feeling absorbed into relational depth. The description of aliveness echoes this telling through the body. For some therapists, it is an '*indicator of knowing that a point is being reached in contact*', communication, or relational depth. It is a felt sense rather than an articulated one. One therapist pointed out the difference between existing and living as an important feature of therapy.

Therapists spoke of being very sensory and how this allows a deeper level of knowing; again it's not a cognitive knowing but an experiential way of knowing them. The use of head and heart was articulated to demonstrate the felt difference in the room with clients and self when the therapist is being with rather than trying to do. It was also described as a way to frame, and locate experience. The therapist speaks about techniques being fantastic for accessing that head part and kind of thinking. Here logic and cognition are taken as one way in which we understand and see the world. Seen as useful it plays an important role but when combined with other ways of knowing. That often simply having cognitive understanding does not mean understanding the emotions or feeling them and that the journey in therapy is very valuable not just the outcome.

The therapist reflects on the difference between a still heart and a restless one, noting the impact on their therapeutic work. They discuss experiences of disconnection when their heart isn't still and how training helped them work on intentions. The importance of trust, attunement, and understanding one's agenda in therapeutic connections is emphasised. For the therapist, manualised practices and techniques are discussed, with a focus on adapting them to individual clients and maintaining a still heart.

Support and Supervision

An invaluable aspect of practitioners feeling validated and supported in their work came in the form of supervision and peer support. This made the therapists feel as though they have a voice within the larger work environment. The therapists spoke of the difference between clinical supervisors who have experiences in several modalities versus managers who potentially do not understand the work being carried out and have the organisation as their primary focus. One therapist described a relief to know their manager was a counsellor and therefore could acknowledge the tensions experienced in the work.

Managers who showed concern over targets and outcomes often placed greater pressure on therapists to meet the targets. Metric outcomes were seen as the marker of success and data collection forms often manipulated and changed. Therapists felt that there was not a realistic understanding of how recovery happens. And no space for clients to feel worse before they feel better. The concern was that managers would use the manualised criteria to inform clinical practice and therefore therapists at times felt 'trapped' to present good outcomes whilst hiding that they had adapted the model during an intervention.

Therapists talked through some of their struggles with chaotic systems in government-funded organisations, describing becoming employed but not knowing who their manager was or where they were meant to be. As a supervisor, another therapist described how scary it is for trainees to go out there and start working if they don't have the core counselling skills. They describe their work as trying to help address the balance for the supervisees and how restrictions can bring about ethical issues for practice.

References

Ayton, D. Tsindos, T. Berkovic, D. (2023). *Qualitative research – A practical guide for health and social care researchers and practitioners*. Monash University. Clayton, Victoria, Australia

Blaxter, L. Hughes. C. Tight. M. (2001). *How to research* (2nd ed.). Philadelphia, PA: Open University Press.

Bogdan, R. Biklen, S. K. (2007). *Qualitative research for education: An introduction to theories and methods* (5th ed.). Pearson. Boston, Massachusetts (MA), USA

De Beauvoir, S. (1947/1976). *The ethics of ambiguity*. Trans: Frechtman, B. New York: Citadel Press.

Eagleton, T. (2008). *Literary theory an introduction*. Oxford: Blackwell Publishing.

Giorgi, A. (2009). *The descriptive phenomenological method in psychology: A modified Husserlian approach*. Pittsburgh, PA: Duquesne University Press.

Giorgi, A. (1997). The theory, practice, and evaluation of the phenomenological method as a qualitative research procedure. *Journal of Phenomenological Psychology*. Vol. 28 (2), pp. 235–260. https://doi.org/10.1163/156916297X00103

Hastings, W. (2010). Research and the ambiguity of reflexivity and ethical practice. *Discourse: Studies in the Cultural Politics of Education*. Vol. 31 (3), 307–318. https://doi.org/10.1080/01596301003786902

Heidegger, M. (1977). *The question concerning technology and other essays*, pp. 3–35. Trans: Lovitt. New York: Harper Textbooks.

Loewenthal, D. (2020). Critical existential-analytic, rather than 'evidence based', psychotherapies: Some implications for practices, theories and research. *European Journal of Psychotherapy and Counselling*. Vol. 22 (1–2), pp. 1–8. https://doi.org/10.1080/13642537.2020.1767845

Moustakas, C. E. (1994). *Phenomenological research methods*. Thousand Oaks, CA: Sage.

Moustakas, C. (1990). *Heuristic research: Design, methodology, and applications*. London: Sage.

Packer, M. J. Addison, R. B. (1989). *Entering the circle: Hermeneutic investigation in psychology*. Albany: State University of New York Press.

People, K. (2021). *How to write a phenomenological dissertation. A step-by-step guide*. Sage Publications. Thousand Oaks, California (CA), USA

Saxon, D. Firth, N. Barkham, M. (2017). The relationship between therapist effects and therapy delivery factors: Therapy modality, dosage, and non-completion. *Administration and Policy in Mental Health*. Vol. 44 (5), pp. 705–715. https://doi.org/10.1007/s10488-016-0750-5

Smith, K. R. (2009). Psychotherapy as Applied Science or Moral Praxis: The Limitations of Empirically Supported Treatment. Journal of Theoretical and Philosophical Psychology, 29(1), 34–46. Washington, DC

Stiegler, B. (1994/1998). Technics and Time, 1: The Fault of Epimetheus (R. Beardsworth & G. Collins, Trans.). Stanford University Press. Stanford, California

Streubert-Speziale, H. J. Carpenter, D. R. (2007). *Qualitative research in nursing: Advancing the humanistic imperative*. Philadelphia, PA: Lippincott Williams and Wilkins.

Vickery, M. R. (1990). Rhetorical maintenance of technological society: Commercial nuclear power and social orthodoxy. In M. J. Medhurst, A. Gonzalez, & T. R. Peterson (Eds.), Communication and the culture of technology (pp. 137–155). Washington State University Press. Pullman, Washington (WA), USA

Wampold, B. E. Baldwin, S. A. Holtforth, M. G. Imel, Z. E. (2017). What characterizes effective therapists? In: Castonguay, L. G. Hill, C. E (Eds.), *How and why are some therapists better than others? Understanding therapist effects*, pp. 37–53. American Psychological Association. Washington, DC, USA

Warren, J. T. Townsend, C. Quigley, L. (2022). Features of depersonalization: An examination and expansion of the cognitive-behavioral model. *Psychology of Consciousness: Theory, Research, and Practice*. Advance online publication. https://doi.org/10.1037/cns0000336

Willig, C. (2008). *Introducing qualitative research in psychotherapy: Adventures in theoryand method* (2nd ed.). Maidenhead: Open University Press.

7

OPEN TO POSSIBILITIES

Introduction

What has become increasingly clear throughout this book is the way in which manualised approaches within funded therapies and within the paradigm of EBP have reconfigured not only therapeutic practice but also the personal identity and lived experience of therapists. Within institutional frameworks, procedural fidelity and measurable outcomes have become an authority over relational and contextual dimensions. This creates tensions between institutional authority and clinical judgement, which often results in therapists navigating away from specific models or institutions which audit adherence to prescribed protocols. This becomes more evident within hierarchical systems when therapists feel implicit threat or punitive consequences under the guise of upholding standards and accountability. This was felt acutely for therapists when initially training and trying to build one's own style in practice. Accounts gathered start to build a picture of a system which instils fear of failure and which uses an audit culture to reprimand individual practice despite high levels of qualification, whilst simultaneously failing to provide adequate resources and to bridge over the ideal conditions from which the models are tested.

As manualised models are commonly presented as the safest and most '*legitimate*' ways to practise within institutions, there is often little room for adaptions, any form of questioning, or a responsiveness to unique individual therapeutic encounters. This leaves us with a conundrum, when drawing from the lived experience of practitioners, there was a strong sentiment across the board that tools, techniques, and frameworks are most helpful when used as a creative component of the process. Therapists found techniques and tools as highly valuable when consciously used and rooted in the context of therapy. Therapists felt that their intuition and felt sense within the therapeutic relationship was a source of knowledge which guided if techniques would be used. Therapist were better able to dialogue with the use of a technique to see if it was hindering or opening

DOI: 10.4324/9781003651666-7

possibilities for the client. Therefore indicating that techniques and tools, even manualised interventions are not in themselves inherently problematic. It is the way they are used and implemented which appears to cause difficulties. Restrictive environments, interventions, timeframes, and institutional demands all played a role in overriding the therapist's responsiveness and connectivity to the practice rendering them powerless to move with intuition. Therapists reported feelings of guilt for adapting models to better meet the needs of their clients, suggesting how institutional norms can exert a powerful moral force which shapes people both internally and externally. This aligns back with ideas of how interventions are integrated into societal networks of power (Guilfoyle, 2008). While some critics argue that adaptation undermines reliability and threatens the validity of evidence-based outcomes, the findings suggest that therapists adapt precisely because the intervention, as designed, is often unworkable in real-world contexts. In such cases, strict adherence risks becoming not only ineffective but ethically questionable.

Therapists who could fall back on other modalities were able to confidently balance techniques within the therapeutic encounter, whilst therapists who had learnt to deliver interventions with no therapeutic background found additional pressures to make the therapy '*fit*' the model. This additionally showed up in training as therapists reported moral and ethical conflicts between a commitment to client welfare and a compliance to procedure. One therapist failed their assessment for deviating from the model as they attended to a client's distress. Their previous training as a psychotherapist conflicted with what was being asked and eventually, they stopped adhering to the model to be with the client, a frightening echo of Milgram's study in the 1960s.

What has become clear is the issues faced on an institutional level and the reluctance of institutions to permit deviation from manualised practice, even when such deviation is clinically justified (Waller, Stringer and Mayer, 2012).

This chapter is divided into two parts, the first explores the ethical tensions across interconnected dimensions of the personal, practicum, and political. This brings together some of the complexities faced when manualised interventions mediate relationships and institutions limit professional agency to help models adapt. The second part considers how design of research and environments can play a helpful role in rethinking possibilities for the future of psychotherapeutic practice, which touches on the need for infrastructure, diversity, and a critical stance as the corner stone of change.

Ethics

Aligning with Loewenthal's (2020) distinction between implications and applications, we begin to see that the ethical practice does not reside in universal processes or rigid methodologies, but rather it can be found in the capacity to engage thoughtfully with knowledge while remaining open to uncertainty and the emergence of the other. This orientation resists the facelessness of systems and challenges the third-party political and economic forces that increasingly shape psychotherapy. In doing so, it invites therapists to remain ethically engaged not only within the therapeutic dyad but also within the broader structures that govern their work. This forces a form of activism within psychotherapy when following one's own practice and experience becomes an automatic challenge to the system and institution. In many cases, therapists feel bound by the authority of the institution they worked in and in turn felt compelled to prioritise procedure over practice. This could be seen in training institutions and work environments which repeatedly overrode the judgement of the clinical. In each case, the practitioner felt there would be consequences to not following protocol.

In the case of trainees, a feeling of inadequate authority to question or adjust the interventions meant a stifling of their learning and erosion of confidence in practice. Trainees who had already trained as counsellors felt a sense of guilt to continue despite their want to adjust to the client. Throughout the interviews, ethical issues emerged concerning therapists' tendency to appease institutional requirements, even when doing so conflicted with what was considered clinically appropriate. This reinforces the idea that there is a prerogative for institutions not to allow their trainees to deviate from the manualised practice (Waller, Stringer and Mayer, 2012).

Therapists felt that manualised practices could be integrated into practice as a useful tool but should not become the full practice. Therefore, space for adaptation plays a significant role in giving therapists a freedom to be responsive and in the moment whilst still having manualised interventions as part of the practice. Some argue that the adaptation is problematic and affects the reliability of results as interventions cannot be properly assessed; however, all the findings suggested that therapists made adaptations because the intervention was not possible and therefore ineffective in its application. There were moments encountered in the findings when therapists felt a sense of ethical responsibility towards their clients in relation to fulfilling the course of treatment but even with such intentions, the reality of changing dynamics, needs, and risk often meant a relocation onto a new waiting list.

As we can see, there are systematic problems relating to evidence and its lack of incorporating changes that the therapists make. This became evident as therapists would often talk about not telling people or worried about being monitoring if not following the process as given. Therapists fear punitive action if there is a failure to justify and demonstrate their actions, despite their actions being situationally responsive and relational. In highly manualised practice, therapists worried about making more space for their clients and the impact of assessments and waiting lists on their clients.

Therapists practised in a technical and non-technical manner but acknowledged that there is an ethical imperative to become aware of the choices made and to not follow blindly. We must be responsible for our own well-being as the system is not designed to care for therapists, rather it is designed to utilise them for deliverable outcomes. Therapists need the space to manoeuvre accordingly whether they wish to or not; that choice should be theirs is theirs.

It is important to remember that technology is considered an 'applied science', and as such, there is often a turning to the expert researcher or developer for answers which might belong to a more democratic participation in its design (Winner, 1995). What is meant by this is that there is a moral and ethical gap between those who create the intervention and those who use it. Therefore, this makes us ask practitioners what is and isn't working, so that psychotherapy can be more adaptable (Mearns and Cooper, 2020; Murphy, 2013).

Practice Dimension

Several factors consistently showed themselves to be highly significant in relation to practice. Both in theory and in the findings, the therapeutic relationship served as the most impactful vehicle of change. We are left with the concept that technologies such as standardised techniques do not solely work as arbitrary tools to fulfil our agenda but help towards constituting the interaction. We are encouraged to ask, not only what a technology or technique can do but also how it might influence our being in the room and acknowledge how our interactions have been mediated.

Evidence-based practice is geared around efficacy but does not always translate over to *'real-world'* application. The therapist therefore often plays a vital facilitatory role which balances many factors in understanding a relationship that is often multidimensional and deeply rich in connectivity. However, with manualised interventions this role is often lacking with recognition, space, training, and support which are all integral to such a complex engagement. Another aspect to consider is how resources are increasingly unrealistic for the therapists. They often do not have the resources, time, or even people to carry out the intervention. The practice gap appears to become increasingly wider, the more manualised an intervention becomes. Certain aspects cannot be accounted for in the room such as intuition of when to carry out a technique or practice.

The physical aspect is one of the more notable and significant parts of the findings. As the intervention becomes increasingly manualised the more disconnected from the self and other the therapist becomes. With this form a practice becomes dependent on the external interventions as the praxis of the therapist becomes externalised. With such an array of interventions and techniques therapists are at times faced with feelings of inadequacy and for some there is an erosion of confidence. There is a willingness and openness to learning from practice, theory, peer, supervision, groups, and clients from therapists. There is a hunger from therapists for robust and secure learning environments which offer a sense of community, learning, and a diversity of thought and voice. Yet in the healthcare sector, therapists are met with a world of audit, managerialism, overwhelming caseloads, and a disconnect from a very personal endeavour to be with others. There is always some form of technology at play, mediating the therapy room whether it be words, methods, or theories. We too as human beings are capable of being a technology in our own right; our perception and eyes, history, and experience all shape us and our view of the world, but it is the openness with which we approach a situation that offers growth and development.

With the '*real-world*' application of interventions being problematic at times, failings in the therapy are frequently taken on as a lack in the therapist. Punitive auditing practices add a layer of apprehension and pressure for the therapists to gain results from interventions. There is a tendency to blame themselves if their confidence is low which stood out as a contradiction for the researcher. In one moment, the therapists would be describing how they found restrictive practices as a hindrance in the therapy. Simultaneously, they also blamed themselves for potentially not carrying out the process properly.

As we have seen throughout the chapters and findings, there is little doubt of the impact and influence the industrialisation of psychotherapy has had on practice (Jackson and Rizq, 2019). Highlighted is the entwined relationship between the therapeutic encounter and the economic, political, and social demands placed on the practice of psychotherapy. Working environments which employ therapists are often subject to these larger constructs, and as such, they themselves often put a demand on the therapist to produce outcomes. Evident in the findings were the difficulties faced by therapists in statutory services belonging to the NHS, in particular 'Child and Adolescent Mental Health Services' (CAMHS), NHS talking therapies, all of which are under immense pressure to evidence their worth through outcomes. The battle for funding among other organisations and charities has also produced the need to evidence outcomes, but as we have seen in the findings, therapists are often adapting models without anyone knowing and so there is an automatic gap in accuracy towards outcomes. In addition, services which select their clients under very specific criteria have an advantage over services that work with anyone who comes for support in relation to outcome.

Personal and Political Dimension

One finding which resonated was in relation to a personal engagement and the tension held between being oneself in the therapy room and being or showing up as a therapist in the therapy room. Every therapist interviewed took up the profession from a personal desire to engage, better understand, and support others. Their practice emerged and was heavily rooted in their personal history. What was missed most in highly manualised practice was the personal self. At the more intensive levels, therapists describe a personal loss of self in the process. This repeated loss of self appeared to have an impact not solely on the well-being of therapists but on their practice and career. The book has explored how a fusion of horizons can shape and reconstitute a therapist giving them a sense of ongoing growth. Therapists could be detrimentally impacted if too tightly restricted and unable to develop not just as a practitioner but as a person. There appears a marked difference between the experience of sharing a space and lending oneself to that space versus taking up a space on behalf of targets and outcomes.

However, manualised practice was also encountered as being a protective layer for therapists with increasing caseloads of highly vulnerable young people. With high risk levels and strong safeguarding protocols, the therapist appreciated highly manualised approaches as they allowed her to practise in a way that staved off burn out. This lean towards professionalisation and dependency on the very systems which apply the pressure is part of what Weber and Heidegger alert us to in the chapters. Another therapist interviewed has spoken about her preference to work in a more embodied full way which was also highly relevant in the findings. Therapists felt they were not utilising all their abilities or '*full self*' as some would term. There is a connection identified between the therapist's confidence and validation with their sense of autonomy. The findings aligned with research that found how practitioners felt they needed strong peer networks, practitioner-oriented research and books, and a sense of value towards clinical experience to improve (Chamless, Steward and Stirman, 2012).

Therapists felt they would have to adapt because models of practice were not broad enough to incorporate what was emerging in the therapeutic relationship. But as we saw for some, there was a sense that they might be doing something wrong if adapting the model. Despite being trained as a psychoanalyst and feeling that the process would be detrimental to her young person, one therapist describes adapting the model as '*rule breaking*' but justifies her actions by stating it was a child-focussed decision. It is argued that her decision was an ethical one, she engaged in a way that was context relevant and unique to the situation (Finlay, 2009). Here sits a core problem, how have we reached a point in which highly qualified clinicians responding ethically makes them feel they are doing something wrong.

What is emerging here is a conversation about how the political agendas and systems of services and organisations instruct the therapist rather than learn from the therapist. Therapists are increasingly used for their technical abilities for eternal systems rather than the relationship.

A recurring theme throughout was a fear of disclosure. Therapists spoke of not informing supervisors or institutions about the adaptations they made, worried about monitoring, or punitive responses. There appears a culture of silence which reveals a systemic problem that has previously been highlighted, that evidence is often generated without accounting for the realities of practice. Often, the gap between prescribed models and lived clinical realities creates conditions in which therapists internalise responsibility for systemic failures; they take accountability and allocate blame to themselves when interventions fall short. This is particularly evident in highly manualised services where assessments, waiting lists, and outcome measures dominate the therapeutic landscape, further constraining the relational space. Behind this sits an even bigger problem, the idea of blame and failure being treated as locatable in a relational situation rather than explored and understood. That rupture becomes something to be feared rather than to be worked with. These subtle shifts rob therapists of encounters which may be helpful to their learning and development by sidestepping deeper therapeutic work. Taking Merleau-Ponty's (2017) view that the body is the primary sight of knowing and that the body learns skills which shape how the body responds to given situations, there is a danger that we become habitual in our practices. We risk developing a predisposition to acting in repeatable ways despite being presented with various possibilities, treating the body as a limited object in the world rather understanding that it holds within it a world of possibilities for action within different environments.

Designing Environments for Therapeutic Practice

Whilst there is clearly an attempt to work at the most cost-effective and time-effective way possible, this book suggest that this becomes ineffective in the long term as a revolving door for clients is created. Through a lack of support and an increasing pressure to resolve any aspect of the client's difficulties can often have a trickle-down effect. Therapists showed through the interviews that they can adapt to conditions and work within certain parameters, where they start to struggle if all the space in the therapy room is used up for external agendas. Under some conditions, the intervention could not possibly work, and as such, therapists often took on the blame despite their attempts to meet all the needs both externally and in the therapy room.

Therapists responded best to environments in which others shared their difficulties such as peer support, clinical supervisors, and training in which personal struggle and practices are discussed. Environments which offered a personalisation and flexibility were able to sustain and hold on to therapists. Work environments which were demanding and process led rather than people led, often saw its therapist leave and move predominantly into private practice or less restrictive workplaces. This felt the same in relation to training and to continued professional development. Organisations that offered therapists to share their views and their take on practices prompted deeper and more fulfilling engagement. More so is a sense of validation in which the therapist can trust themselves and respond to the situation at hand.

Therapists are not machines and tools from which to produce a conveyor belt service for people, and psychotherapy is not a quick fix to undesirable situations. There is a culture emerging of fast paced in and out services which are under immense pressure to see people and provide a service. We know that the therapeutic relationship offers a space from which change can occur and that given the right conditions, a person is able to access something within themselves that feels strong and adaptive. The same should be provided for therapists, there should be a space within the work environment which helps and promotes therapists to access their capabilities in a strong and validating way rather than placing demands. It is appreciated that organisations are overwhelmed, and it is precisely this reason that we look to the political for support as opposed to placing greater demand to produce. In essence, organisations should find ways of protecting therapists from these huge external demands and protect the therapeutic relationship.

Recommendations for more flexible working environments and idiosyncratic practices may seem an obvious starting point; however, there is still a struggle to implement this. One issue may be the lack of infrastructure available. As we saw in previous chapters, infrastructure played a key role in synergising a movement. To counterbalance, psychotherapy would benefit from understanding where infrastructure has failed to offer alternative platforms which loosen the dependency on the political and economic. Therapists need to feel supported in their stance to resist harmful practices. Through diverse dialogue, research, practice workshop, diverse voices, and a sense of protective community, there are opportunities for therapists to speak openly and candidly. Much of this work is already taking place but there is not the same synergy without the connective tissue of infrastructure to help bring it together.

A Call for Diversity in Therapeutic Knowledge

Offering a varied and diverse learning system is a practice of fusion. Offering therapists experiences which allow them to move from their situated position allows for flexibility in practice and an opportunity to explore oneself through a different encounter. Critical thinking modules on training courses are of high value but are increasingly filtered out for modules in specific practices and skills. There is a call to return the critical to the forefront of practice and allow the challenge in research to become a body of knowledge. The art of maintaining a critical or questioning stance helps fluidity as it always remains open to possibility. Therefore, the practice of being with otherness is an essential quality which cannot be taught directly in training but can be encouraged in practice. Spaces for the experiential component of being a therapist feel essential with the increase in number of therapists and supervisors who have never experienced therapy or delved into their own otherness. These therapeutic journeys for people could very possibly be just as, if not more, valuable than a certificate.

As we have seen through various means, the therapist learns through a combination of processes such as academic training, peer support, praxis, and supervision. Within all these domains there needs to be a level of engagement and openness for a '*fusion of horizons*' to take place. In this sense, breaching self-evidence and finding one's own language can feel an intimidatingly vulnerable place to be. This is not the place to be met with targets and punitive practices as we have seen happen. There are of course mandates and expectations which organisations both public and private aim to fulfil. This, however, does not mean that a negotiation of space and openness cannot be met. The findings showed quite the opposite, therapists who were given space felt more inclined to stay in their role, enjoyed their work, and felt able to engage with clients in a meaningful and transformative way despite there being targets. Therefore, institutions are hindering a huge resource when they limit professional agency, with ramifications to self and practice. There is an erosion of confidence as validating systems encourage adherence over the critical. There are few places to feedback, integrate, or feel supported to make a stance against issues as they arise in psychotherapeutic work. There is a need to embrace the '*critical*' over the '*evidential*' through research and practice. An aspect of doing so involves developing the ability to feed back into the system, to bring transparency and challenging voice which does not become an anomaly to be fixed within the system but indeed becomes incorporated as a shaping force.

More than ever, openness and diversity within communities is needed to foster diversity in knowledge. Through dialogue and being with others, we are encouraged to not only hear the voices of others but to hear our own dialogues and encounter other values. As Christopher suggests, this is important because "*Cross-cultural contact not only reveals important differences in how individuals think, feel, and act, but in what they aspire to*" (2001. p. 125). This requires a level of uncertainty and an environment which challenges through questions rather than directives of how to be. One recommendation would be to create spaces where hierarchical elements such as management or assessors are removed for therapeutic peer support. Incorporating and designing spaces into training, peer, research, and institutions helps the fluidity of knowledge past between practitioners, whilst actively reshaping the audit culture.

Incorporating an 'Ethical' Dimension in the Design of Manualised Interventions

By exploring manualised interventions as a form of technology, the research was able to delve into the philosophy of technology which is an ever-expanding discipline and offers helpful applications to other disciplines. It shares with therapy, a focus on the ethical dimension of technology and the ways in which it shapes the world and individuals around us. Post-phenomenological enquiries into the role of technology have allowed this book to open the door to a different way of viewing manualised interventions. Rather than placing any inherent value of good or bad, it views technology as one way to see the world rather than the only way to see the world. This means we can instead focus on the experience it offers to its users. By exploring the experiences of therapists, we have been able to consider manualised practices in a different way from the evidence-based protocol which currently dominate. We have come to see that there is a network of connectedness to the environment which must be considered and that isolated measurements of techniques are inadequate for the level of complexity and more prone to being a subtext truth rather than a reality.

In essence, there is an interest to further consider research which explores interventions not solely from a symptom reduction perspective as an example but also from a mediation perspective. The experiences that take place between clients and therapists can leave a lasting impression both positively and negatively. Therefore, it is important to diversify therapeutic research beyond the room and explore external pressures placed on the therapy. Therapeutic models have a blueprint available to them through the philosophy of technology which is a starting point for incorporating ethics. This could play a role in expanding the current blueprint within the medical model.

References

Chamless, D. Stewart, R. Stirman, S. (2012). A qualitative investigation of practicing psychologists' attitudes toward research-informed practice: Implications for dissemination strategies. *Professional Psychology: Research and Practice*. Vol. 43 (2), pp. 100–109.

Christopher, J. (2001). Culture and psychotherapy: Toward a hermeneutic approach. *Psychotherapy*. Vol. 38 (2), pp. 115–128.

Finlay, L. (2009). Debating phenomenological research methods. *Phenomenology and Practice*. Vol. 3, pp. 6–25.

Guilfoyle, M. (2008). CBT'S integration into societal networks of power. *European Journal of Psychotherapy and Counselling*. Vol. 10 (3), pp. 197–206.

Jackson, C. Rizq, R. (2019). *The industrialisation of care: Counselling, psychotherapy and the Impact of IAPT*. PCCS Books. Monmouth, United Kingdom

Loewenthal, D. (2020). Critical existential-analytic, rather than 'evidence based', psychotherapies: Some implications for practices, theories and research. *European*

Journal of Psychotherapy and Counselling. Vol. 22 (1–2), pp. 1–8. https://doi.org/10.1080/13642537.2020.1767845

Mearns, D. Cooper, M. (2020). *Working at relational depth in counselling and psychotherapy* (2nd ed.). London: Sage Publications Ltd.

Merleau-Ponty, M. (2017). *Phenomenology of perception*. Trans: Smith, C. London: Forgotten Books.

Murphy, D. (2013). Mutuality and relational depth in counselling and psychotherapy. In: Knox, R. Murphy, D. Wiggins, S. Cooper, M. Knox, R. (Eds.), *Relational depth: New perspectives and developments*, pp. 185–195. New York: Palgrave Macmillan.

Waller, G. Stringer, H. Mayer, C. (2012). What cognitive behavioural techniques do therapists report using when delivering cognitive behaviour therapy for the eating disorder? *Journal of Consulting and Clinical Psychology*. Vol. 80 (1), pp. 171–175.

Winner, L. (1995). Citizen virtues in a technological order. In: Feenberg, A. Hannay, A. (Eds.), *Technology and the politics of knowledge*, pp. 65–84. Bloomington: Indiana University Press.

8

CONCLUSION

This book began as a question which emerged from practice and an observation of psychotherapy over the years shifting towards practices which felt harmful to therapists and clients. With a deep curiosity to explore how and why this was potentially happening, there appeared a community of people who also felt this increasing shift towards managed, calculable, and technological ways of being in psychotherapy. Resistances and debates are held on multiple levels within the divide on ideology and paradigms of methods. This book takes interest and is aimed at getting behind the scenes of methodologies to explore the mechanisms which drive towards a particular direction. At the heart of this book is our understanding or at times lack of understanding towards the way we have come to relate with and to technology. By drawing manualised interventions within a broader philosophical understanding of technology, we are afforded a new perspective on the way technics in psychotherapy bring huge implications for therapeutic encounters.

Throughout the book, we have explored how, over the past decade, psychotherapy has become shaped by systems of manualised interventions, and evidence-based protocols in the name of '*best practice*'. Whilst models of practice appear to be driven by well-intentioned goals of consistency, and accessibility, problems have arisen within the institutional delivery of these models in funded therapies. We have seen how the economic, social, and political agendas are severed by a particular interpretation of technology, the instrumental. Psychotherapy is increasingly becoming the tool by which people shape themselves rather than discovering and encountering their possibilities through a relational unfolding. Symptoms have become something to be rid of rather than understood, bypassing the social pressures placed on people as their suffering is seen through an individualistic lens. In turn, psychotherapy risks being conditioned into a technology of social order rather than a diversifying and expanding exploration. Therapists find themselves with less agency as the applied sciences defer authority to '*experts*' and developers which creates amoral and ethical gap

DOI: 10.4324/9781003651666-8

between those who design technologies and those who use them (Winner, 1995). Fundamentally this alters the conditions and practices of therapists and researchers who have dedicated themselves to the vocation. Such practices cause scepticism among practitioners towards non-practitioners dictating practice (Chamberless, Steward and Stirman, 2012).

As part of starting conversations and opening new frameworks to consider the culture of psychotherapy, it felt imperative to offer voices to other practitioners and their experiences within these institutions. Through this, we discovered strong sentiment across the board that tools, techniques, and frameworks are at their most helpful when used as a creative component of the process and not the whole process. One in which therapist and client can create meaning unique to their space. Highly manualised interventions were viewed as negatively impacting the therapeutic relationship and over time having a detrimental effect on the therapist. Practitioners spoke of their development becoming hindered, relational depth being impacted, and an erosion of their confidence within rigid and highly audited working environments. Their inability to feel they could adapt models to be more responsive and relevant meant that they became ethically conflicted. When conditions became too hostile in work environments, a lack of agency to challenge the system meant that therapists often felt leaving was the only option in harsh working environments. Furthermore, this shows how the systems and institutions often don't adapt but instead remove or force out the anomaly, passing up learning opportunities.

What becomes evident is that there is a difficulty in assessing the experience of manualised practice without considering the wider context of the environment. These aspects emerge as paramount and integrate with the experience and the practice itself. Findings implied that the higher the level of manualised intervention, the more likely this served wider organisational systems as opposed to the therapy itself. This brings to the forefront the importance of acknowledging our relationship with method and technique, as part of an ethical engagement with our practice.

Therefore, what is advocated for is a practice of critical engagement with our relationship to method and techniques in research and practice. It is an encouragement that we continue running the borders of theory and practice in the hope that we can attempt to have some awareness of our '*embeddedness*' to the situation which presents. This requires that we acknowledge how we are in some ways always entangled in method, theory, and practice rather than separate from it (Willig, 2008). In this sense, '*efficacy*' is not an arbitrary tool that simply provides a clinician with the best available data. It is also a shaping force that is shifting the very culture of psychotherapy when we allow '*efficacy*' to favour the system over the people within it. We must become aware of when structured support becomes stifled support and what it means for us to engage in technology.

What has emerged is a need to recognise that the therapist has '*technê*' in their '*Being*' as does the client, as such there is a world of potentiality to create and encounter through articulating one's own language. The idea that therapists participate in carrying out therapeutic interventions which are externally provided requires a blind trust in the functionality of the system (Stiegler, 1994). But as of late, we have started to see the systems like IAPT begin to malfunction for people and at some point, we must ask if we are starting to do more harm than good (Davies, 2022).

We are encouraged to take up this engagement and accept the task of ambiguity and complexity of each given moment as part of our being and ethical approach (De Beauvoir, 1947/1976). We understand that methods and techniques within psychotherapy are not static disconnected tools, but rather they play a role within a larger context that is social, political, and economic. Therefore, this presents the case that technique and method can sit as part of and contribute towards a larger construct that may not be immediately apparent to the therapist.

This engagement with technology is the reason why AI has not been discussed in greater detail. As stated in the beginning, the book serves as kindling for larger conversations and also to prepare for those larger conversations. By taking some of the hidden layers away from the detached sense of techniques as instrumental tools, it is hoped that the relationship to methods and technique have been somewhat re-evaluated for the reader. The aim has not been to argue for or against but instead re-engage critical thinking and let people decide for themselves what AI and other technological methods might mean or say about us as individuals and a society.

There is a fluidity to psychotherapy in which its meaning, purpose, and aim can change at different moments and in which the position of the therapist is re-examined and may need to be reconstituted. One central theme which does not alter is a move towards freedom to be oneself and to be a person in the encounter first which manualised interventions can get in the way of. Psychotherapy is a creative and personal endeavour which offers deep authentic connection to the other as a way of alleviating challenges and difficulties faced. Due to this process, personal growth is available to both therapist and client simultaneously. Manualised tools are experienced as useful and helpful in promoting conversations and moving through '*stuckness*' when used intuitively. High levels of rigidness in manualised interventions can conflict with the fluid nature of psychotherapy causing a disconnect to the relationship and the individuals involved. Highly manualised practices are seen as a defence or protection but at the cost of feeling cut off from the self and the other which has an impact on the relationship. There is also an impact to the therapist's sense of individual validation and ability. Highly manualised practices need adaptation by the therapist in some form or another to continue, otherwise they often fall out of use. Agenda is often an indicator to the therapist that signals a wrong turn.

In this sense, '*becoming*' is not a destination but a direction and the reality is nobody has an accurate road map, but some are making very similar journeys and have some insights towards ways in which the body can be a form of compass. But it is not about understanding or grasping the answers as that can be done anytime through being taught. This is a different form of practice, one which allows us to stand back and give space for something unknowable to emerge from which we can learn through a tacit knowledge. In the same light with which we take responsibility for becoming aware of our words and histories, we must also become aware of how our technical applications shape the therapeutic space. There should not be a '*blind faith*' in the name of evidence or science, not because it can't be trusted, quite the contrary, science is capable of remarkable things, but because 'blind faith' encourages a disengagement from the possibilities which are emerging. To remain ethical, the therapist is encouraged to be present and consider theories and evidence as possibilities rather than concrete applications. Through this the therapist can in some way protect the space in the therapy room and as such can leave an open forum without losing the strength their theories have to offer.

This notion of giving space in therapy to allow new emerging encounters feels to be an essential component for practice. And although this may seem contrary to ideas of efficiency and time-bound manualised interventions, there is no advocating dogmatically for one or the other. Instead, this is an attempt to better understand how environmental factors such as training, institutions, management, economy, and technology have shaped our practices. What is being suggested here is that therapists should have autonomy and scope which allows for a response to the given moment and the ability to practice in a way that is intuitive to the space. Here phenomenology offers an alternative to outcome driven or procedural thinking: one in which we can understand psychotherapy as a living and unfolding practice rather than an application of method alongside fulfilling criteria.

Rather than producing or replicating knowledge, can psychotherapy become a space of *unfolding?* What stands out is the way in which this resists the reduction of experience into method or measure. It recognises that both therapist and client participate in the unfolding of meaning and that such meaning is always situated and in motion.

Techniques and methods have been incredibly useful, and developing methodologies in qualitative studies appear to be going from strength to strength. However, it is only with unknowable space that the new and creative aspects of research and practice can emerge. That practice needs to incorporate a space which is ungraspable and unknowable in order that we are moved to open new possibilities for the client and ourselves. Allowing people to unfold in a way that feels held rather than conditioned my technique. There is a great deal to be gained from knowledge but simultaneously there is an endless potential for growth which comes through the process of resisting the immediate knowing and remaining open. Therapy in practice therefore can present as an opportunity for continuous growth and development as each encounter is unique in context and meaning. Each unfolding can and is different if given the space, as Rogers poignantly says:

> People are just as wonderful as sunsets if you let them be. In fact, perhaps the reason we can truly appreciate a sunset is that we cannot control it. When I look at a sunset as I did the other evening, I don't find myself saying, "Soften the orange a bit on the right hand corner..." I don't try to control a sunset. I watch with awe as it unfolds.
>
> *(Rogers, 1980. p. 22)*

References

Chambless, D. L., Stewart, R. E., & Stirman, S. W. (2012). A qualitative investigation of practicing psychologists' attitudes toward research-informed practice: Implications for dissemination strategies. Professional Psychology: Research and Practice, 43(2), 100–109. Washington, DC

Davies, J. (2022). *Sedated how modern capitalism created our mental heath crisis.* Atlantic Books. London, England

De Beauvoir, S. (1947/1976). *The ethics of ambiguity.* Trans: Frechtman, B. New York: Citadel Press.

Rogers, C. (1980). *A way of being.* Houghton Mifflin. Boston, Massachusetts (MA), USA

Stiegler, B. (1994). *Technics and time, 1. The fault of Epimetheus.* Trans: Beardsmorth, R. Collins, G. Stanford, CA: Stanford University Press.

Willig, C. (2008). *Introducing qualitative research in psychotherapy: Adventures in theory and method.* (2nd ed.). Maidenhead: Open University Press.

Winner, L. (1995). Citizen virtues in a technological order. In: Feenberg, A. Hannay, A. (Eds.), *Technology and the politics of knowledge*, pp. 65–84. Bloomington: Indiana University Press.

INDEX

For Product Safety Concerns and Information please contact our EU
representative GPSR@taylorandfrancis.com
Taylor & Francis Verlag GmbH, Kaufingerstraße 24, 80331 München, Germany

www.ingramcontent.com/pod-product-compliance
Ingram Content Group UK Ltd.
Pitfield, Milton Keynes, MK11 3LW, UK
UKHW022344190926
475702UK00015B/2091
9781041096887